FINDING IS THE FIRST ACT

THE SOCIETY OF BIBLICAL LITERATURE
SEMEIA SUPPLEMENTS
William A. Beardslee, Editor
Dan O. Via, Jr., Associate Editor
J. William Whedbee, Associate Editor

FINDING IS THE FIRST ACT

Trove Folktales
and
Jesus' Treasure Parable

by
John Dominic Crossan

FORTRESS PRESS
Philadelphia, Pennsylvania

SCHOLARS PRESS
Missoula, Montana

Library of Congress Cataloging in Publication Data

Crossan, John Dominic.
   Finding is the first act.

   (Semeia supplements; 9 ISSN 0145-3254)
   Bibliography: p.
   Includes index.
   1. Hidden treasure (Parable) 2. Treasure-trove (in religion, folklore, etc.) 3. Tales—
History and criticism. I. Title. II. Series.
   BT378.H54C76   266 '.2 '061   79-9898
   ISBN 0-8006-1509-3

30, 709

7696F79   Printed in the United States of America   1-1509

For
Neal M. Flanagan, O. S. M.,
teacher and friend.

Finding is the first Act
The second, loss,
Third, Expedition for
the 'Golden Fleece.'

Fourth, no Discovery -
Fifth, no Crew -
Finally, no Golden Fleece -
Jason - sham - too.

The Poems of Emily Dickinson
Vol. 2, Pp. 647–48, No. 870.

CONTENTS

Grateful acknowledgement is made to Oxford University Press for permission to quote from *The Works of George Herbert*. Ed. F. E.. Hutchinson. 1941.

The epigraph poem is reprinted by permission of the publishers and the Trustees of Amherst College from *The Poems of Emily Dickinson*. Ed. Thomas H. Johnson. Cambridge, MA.: The Belknap Press of Harvard University Press. Copyright ©1951, 1955 by the President and Fellows of Harvard College. This permission is gratefully acknowledged.

PREFACE

As we begin to dig we find that we are not the first. For all our knowledge of history, we are surprised. Others have dug before us. Did they find it? Did they take it away? How did they hear it was there? Was it there? Was it ever there? Why? What was it, really? Is it still there? What happened to them?
And that, again, is history. Which leaves us in ignorance.
We continue to dig. No one has been before us tomorrow.
And we dig alone. The true present is a place where only one can stand, who is standing there for the first time.

W. S. Merwin (159)

This book is intended as an experiment to test a theory. The general background of the theory is the present situation of biblical studies and the growing conviction that the complete analysis of a biblical text demands both diachronic and genetic study of its causes and effects as well as synchronic and systemic study of its thematic or generic parallels.

The unit chosen for experimentation is Jesus' parable of The Hidden Treasure in Matt 13:44. This story has already received careful diachronic study in the usual terms of both source (Dehandschutter) and redaction criticism (Kingsbury). The theory I wish to test claims that the passage should also receive synchronic study by viewing it synoptically against the proximate background of other Jewish treasure parables and the wider background of the entire treasure tradition in world folklore.

It is necessary here to acknowledge certain decisions from my own earlier work which I am aware of presuming in this present one. First, the textual corpus which concerns me is not that of Matthew but of Jesus. This in no way denies the validity of the former interest but it emphasizes and distinguishes the different focus of my own investigation. I presume the basic validity of the most rigorously methodical and necessarily negative determination of what in the evangelical Jesus tradition actually stems with some security from the historical Jesus himself. My own work has always begun *after* and been based *upon* the corpus of Jesus material established by that historical scholarship which considers the various titular confessions, for example, and especially the Son of Man complex, as interpretations of Jesus from the early communities but not at all as the original language of Jesus himself. Thus, for me, the original context for the parable of The Hidden Treasure is this historically reconstructed corpus of authentic and original Jesus material. The reason I found any further work necessary in such a situation was because those scholars who had so convincingly and even brilliantly established this historical data base of Jesus' actions and dialogues, sayings and stories, seemed to me to have failed rather completely and even dismally in understanding and interpreting what they had so painstakingly reconstructed. The crucial cause for this failure was the fact that *historical* thinking was required for reconstructing the corpus but *literary* appreciation was required for interpreting its meaning.

Presuming the corpus, then, and also presuming the need for a literary interpretation (Crossan, 1973), I would consider the present book to be a companion piece to my earlier probe into the meaning of the Jesus material. In *Raid on the Articulate* a large selection of this data was interpreted in contrast with aphorisms and narratives of a contemporary parabler, Jorge Luis Borges, along lines which were mostly generic. In the present study a different approach is being attempted. One single unit of the Jesus material will be studied against a far larger corpus with which it is not a generic but a thematic unity. Here, then, is the theory. Jesus' story about The Hidden Treasure could be interestingly studied by mapping its plot options against a great synchronic and synoptic map of world treasure folktales. That is the theory and that is the wager.

Why folktales? Folklore studies, as is well known, have often used a diachronic approach that is immediately resonant with traditional biblical approaches.

> By assembling all the known versions of a particular tale, the folklorist seeks to reconstruct the hypothetical original form of the tale. There is, however, no attempt to explain how this original form may have come into being in the first place. Thus there has been a movement away from the early interest in genesis and cause towards an interest in the process of transmission and evolutionary development. But in any case, the study of folklore has remained diachronic (Dundes, 1962a:95).

Although, of course, diachronic biblical studies have usually been more interested in genesis than development and often in the latter only because of the former, their methods have been very similar to that of historical-geographical folklore studies. My own use of folktales has nothing whatsoever to do with the preceding phenomenon. I have chosen folktales primarily because I am interested in treasure stories where plot and plot options are readily visible and where plot emphases have not receded before advanced developments such as psychological characterization or narrative point of view. I needed, in other words, a fairly vast repertoire of inventoried treasure plots, and I needed stories where, like Jesus' own tale, plot was dominant.

Why Jesus' treasure parable? For three reasons that I am aware of. First, as is evident from *In Parables* (33–34) the story has always fascinated me. I had thought, even before the present book's research, that there was something very strange and different about this story but all that struck me heretofore was the way in which its sequence of Finding, Acting, and Buying was in direct opposition to the sequence in some other Jewish treasure plots whose sequence was Buying, Acting, and Finding (Crossan, 1976a:153–58). Second, in recent work on parables there has often been a tendency to concentrate especially on the longer parables of Jesus. I wanted deliberately to move in the opposite direction and to give full emphasis to a very short parable, to a story composed, in Greek, of a single sentence of thirty-one words, and which just barely qualifies for Aristotle's definition of a story as needing a beginning, middle, and end. I also agree with Howard Schwartz (xix) when he claims that, "The basic challenge of the parable is to write a good story in as short a space as possible." Third, this particular parable, in contrast, for example, to that of The Mustard Seed, does not furnish much grist for the diachronic mill of biblical studies. I was deliberately choosing an item which, in isolation from its Matthean context, could hardly sustain a monograph study along the standard lines of tradition criticism.

My gratitude is due DePaul University on two counts. To the Interlibrary Loan Department in general, and to Mary Zimmerman in particular, for locating older and dustier tomes not available even in the Chicago area. And to my colleagues in the Religious Studies Department for reduced teaching assignments in the quarter when writing was ready.

Finally, during the research for this book I had the strange feeling that the teller and the tale were metonymically or metaphorically united. I was searching out the possibilities of treasure searching. Writing and subject seemed to reflect one another. So also, I suppose, the composing of Jesus' parable reflected its own subject. Digging becomes composing becomes interpreting and the hidden treasure is always *meaning*. I also wanted the form of my interpreting to submit in homage to the form of Jesus' composing, to reflect as best I could the original and enduring surprise of what he himself had said. After I had finished the book and was considering this Preface, I came, by pure coincidence, upon the treasure parable which I have placed at its head. It bespeaks not only the continuing validity of the trove tradition and of treasure parables but, much more importantly, it indicates how treasure digging, story composing, and parable interpreting stand perpetually in metonymic or metaphoric relationship with each other.

THEORY

THEORY

I am the angel who dwells in the point where lines fork. Whoever retraces the way of divided things encounters me, whoever descends to the bottom of contradictions runs into me, whoever mingles again what was separated feels my membraned wing brush his cheek!

Italo Calvino (61)

The story must be told and its telling is a record of the choices, inadvertent or deliberate, the author has made from all the possibilities of language.

W. H. Gass (7)

The meaning of every part of the text, the meaning of every one of its constituent events, is determined by the events which might have taken its place without making nonsense of the text as a whole, the events against which it stands out in contrast.

Philip Pettit (46)

All communication rests upon the possibility of *choice*, or selection from a set of alternatives. . . . a linguistic unit, of whatever level, has no meaning in a given context if it is completely predictable in that context.

Information-content varies inversely with probability. The more predictable a unit is, the less meaning it has. And the *less* probable a particular element is, the *more* meaning it has in that context ("element" should here be taken to refer to all the results of "choice", including silence, permitted by the system of communication for particular contexts).

John Lyons (89, 415)

Shannon's proof states that the amount of information that can flow in any noisy circuit (that is, in the presence of random interference) is proportionate to redundancy, and, conversely, that the information value of any one message is proportionate to nonredundancy or to uncertainty (the surprise value of the item).

Monro S. Edmonton (49)

7

A text is meaningful not only in virtue of what it is but also in virtue of what it might have been. The most relevant exponent of the "might have been" of a work of literature is another work of literature.

M. A. K. Halliday (302-3)

At each crossroads of the action sequence, the narrative—it is more appropriate to focus on the narrative, and not on the writer, because our topic is narrative *language*, not the performance of the storyteller—chooses between several possibilities, and this choice involves at any given moment the very future of the story; obviously the story will change according to whether the door on which one has knocked will open or remain closed, etc. . . . It goes without saying that, where an action is faced with an alternative—having this or that consequence—the narrative invariably chooses that from which it profits, i.e., that which *assures its survival as narrative.*

Roland Barthes (7)

In all fictional works, each time a man is confronted with several alternatives, he chooses one and eliminates the others; in the fiction of Ts′ui Pên, he chooses—simultaneously—all of them. *He creates*, in this way, diverse futures, diverse times which themselves also proliferate and fork.

Jorge Luis Borges (26)

EXPERIMENT

I

EXPEDITION:
WORLD TREASURE TALES

Surely there are great hoards of treasure buried by the rich or the
mighty in times of crisis and left forgotten. Why could not one, if he
is clever enough, uncover such a hoard and live like a king?

Stith Thompson (1951:262)

Imagine hidden treasure stories in world folklore as a vast
synchronic system. Imagine the skeletal structure of this huge
synthesis as the plot options which tellers take in working out the
destiny of their tales. Imagine these forking paths as major narrative
possibilities which religions or prophets, societies or individuals,
traditions or rebels select and in so selecting walk down different
paths, knock on different doors, and enter different dwellings.

It is not very difficult to propose such an act of synchronic
imagination but exactly how does one gather and organize the total
corpus of treasure trove stories contained in world folklore? Is it
possible to do this without extensive computerized resources and,
since this is not presently available, is it worthwhile doing anything
else in its absence? My answer and my hope is that, despite the present
impossibility of obtaining any such *absolute* completion for research,
it is both possible and also profitable to settle for *methodical*
completion. It is therefore imperative to describe in some detail my
method of research so that you can use it to assess the validity of
conclusions derived from or after it.

1.1 Corpus and Method

Two major bibliographical tools in folklore studies immediately
suggest themselves as basic resources for finding the needed corpus of
treasure stories.

1.11 *Type and Motif Indexes*

The first source work is Antti Aarne's *Verzeichnis der Märchentypen* of 1910 which has been translated and revised by Stith Thompson as *The Types of the Folktale* in 1928 and again revised and enlarged in 1961. "This classification is concerned with whole tales, those that have an independent tradition" and it has two major restrictions (Aarne-Thompson, 1961:7, 8). First, the choice of *areas* to be indexed. "Students of the tale have long realized that the lands from Ireland to India form an important tradition area where the same stories are found, some of them extending over the entire territory, and some following these peoples as they migrate to distant continents. Strictly then, this work might be called 'The Types of the Folk-tale of Europe, West Asia, and the Lands Settled by These Peoples.'" Second, the choice of *genres* and *sources* to be indexed, since "this index does not include local legends (German *Sagen*), nor unless they also appear in oral tradition, the great literary collections."

For my own purpose I have not been able to make much use of this type-index. The problem is not so much the two restrictions just mentioned but the very nature of the index which is simply not useful for work on the parable of Jesus which is the focal point of this monograph. An example may clarify this point.

Type No. 1645 is summarized as follows (Aarne-Thompson, 1961:469): "*The Treasure at Home.* A man dreams that if he goes to a distant city he will find treasure on a certain bridge. Finding no treasure, he tells his dream to a man who says that he too has dreamed of treasure at certain place. He describes the place, which is the first man's home. When the latter returns home he finds the treasure." Versions of this tale are indexed from Lithuania, Sweden, Iceland, Scotland, Ireland, Wales, England, France, Spain, Holland, Germany, Czechoslovakia, Hungary, Greece, Turkey, and Japan. If, for example, Jesus had told a parable using some variant of this tale-type, the Aarne-Thompson index would be very important to pose either historical or structural considerations. One might wonder, diachronically, how Jesus' version fitted into the historical-geographical spread of the story, what had caused it and what it had caused. Or, synchronically, one could map the precise content of Jesus' version against all other available ones and thus indicate more clearly the point of his particular version. But there is no tale-type of hidden treasure in the entire Aarne-Thompson index which is even remotely similar to Jesus' story and, accordingly, for my own particular and present purpose, I was not able to get much assistance from that tale-type index nor from any of the others created on its model.

This brought me to the second major source work, to a *motif*-index instead of a *type*-index. In 1932–36 Stith Thompson created a massive *Motif-Index of Folk-Literature*, and he revised and enlarged it in 1955–58. He avoided the two restrictions of the Aarne type-index as follows (Thompson, 1966: 1.10, 11). First, he argued that, "Outside of Europe . . . Aarne's index is of little use. In the remoter parts of the world, whither any adequate study must lead us, the European tale-types are applicable to very few stories. Yet there is much common matter in the folk-literature of the world. The similarities consist not so often in complete tales as in single motifs. Accordingly, if an attempt is made to reduce the traditional narrative material of the whole earth to order (as, for example, the scientists have done with the world-wide phenomena of biology) it must be by means of a classification of single motifs—those details out of which full-fledged narratives are composed." Second, just as there must be no restriction of area, so neither should there be ones of genre or source. The index intends "to arrange in a single logical classification the elements which make up traditional narrative literature. Stories that have formed part of a tradition, whether oral or literary, find a place here. The folktale, the myth, the ballad, the fable, the medieval romance, the fabliau, the jest, the exemplum, and the local tradition have all been included, though some of these divisions have been inadequately recorded. In general, I have used any narrative, whether popular or literary, so long as it has formed a strong enough tradition to cause its frequent repetition." Thus, while type-indexes focus on whole stories, motif-indexes concentrate on their smaller components, on those traditional elements which make up the larger entities recognizable as specific types. I shall return to these motifs and to some of the problems involved in their theoretical delineation in the next section on "Motif and Motifeme." But for now it will suffice to note that motif rather than type-indexes form the essential bibliographical resources for my present experiment.

1.12 *Motif Indexes before 1955–58*

Stith Thompson divided his index, pragmatically rather than theoretically, into twenty-three (A to Z except for I, O, and Y) major categories. "The classification is for the practical purpose of arranging and assorting narrative material so that it can be easily found. In that respect it most resembles a library classification, where books great and small appear together on the shelves: all that matters is that the items belong to the same division and subdivision of human knowledge" (Thompson, 1951:423–24). So we find the classification, "N500–N599. Treasure trove" in his system (Thompson, 1966:5.110–19).

I am accepting, then, *all and only* those numbers given in Thompson's N500s as the *methodically complete* corpus of treasure motifs useful for my experiment.

It is necessary, however, to note three points concerning Thompson's index and the extent of the treasure category in his N500s. First, there is a vast web of cross-references from the N500s to other motif-numbers where treasure concerns appear. In fact there was one awful moment at the start of my research where I thought it possible that every single motif-number might lead through successive cross-references to every other number in the entire multi-volumed set. Second, there are also cross-references to the Aarne-Thompson type-index (and vice versa, now). Third, between the first edition of Thompson's index in 1932–36 and the enlarged revision in 1955–58 many other folklore scholars created motif-indexes using its basic classification system. For example, either as dissertations at Indiana University under Stith Thompson or independently, indexes appeared for Irish (Cross), West Indian (Flowers), Anglo-American (Baughman), Talmudic-Midrashic (Neuman [Noy]), Japanese (Ikeda), and Icelandic (Boberg) materials, to name just a few. In his second and enlarged edition Thompson gave cross-references to all these new motif-indexes so that, in effect, his own work has now become both index and index of indexes.

These three points, these three systems of cross-references, render the nine pages of his N500s vastly larger and considerably more formidable than at first glance.

1.13 *Motif Indexes since 1955–58*

For the period prior to 1958, then, my only resource is Thompson's index for the category of N500–N599 with its huge web of cross-references to other motif-numbers touching tangentially on treasure trove. What of the period between 1958 and the present day?

For this period I have used three major sources. First, and most important, I checked all the motif or type-and-motif indexes noted in my terminal bibliography and dated since 1958. Second, I checked both the "Cumulative Index" attached to the *Abstracts of Folklore Studies* (1963–75) and Alan Dundes' *Folklore Theses and Dissertations in the United States* (to 1976). Third, and primarily because, like most recent folktale collections, they include motif as well as type and subject indexes at the back, I also checked the volumes so far published in the series "Folktales of the World" under the general editorship of Richard M. Dorson.

In summary, then, my method has two successive steps. First, to go through all the motif-indexes presently available and check both the N500s and all cross-references. Second, to find all the sources there indicated except where language and/or location blocked further access. I am convinced that the data base thus arrived at is spread widely enough across historical periods, geographical areas, and literary genres to make the entire experiment worthwhile.

1.2 Motif and Motifeme

One can find books in a library without having to agree with, disagree with, or even discuss the logic of their classification system. Similarly, I am using motif-indexes primarily for practical purposes and do not intend to get any deeper into theoretical discussion than this single section on motif and motifeme.

Stith Thompson (1966:1.19) has noted that, "When the term *motif* is employed, it is always in a very loose sense, and is made to include any of the elements of narrative structure." More specifically (1951:415–16), he has defined his *motif* as "the smallest element in a tale having a power to persist in tradition. In order to have this power it must have something unusual and striking about it. Most motifs fall into three classes. First, are the actors in a tale—gods, or unusual animals, or marvelous creatures like witches, ogres, or fairies, or even conventionalized human characters like the favourite youngest child or the cruel stepmother. Second come certain items in the background of the action—magic objects, unusual customs, strange beliefs, and the like. In the third place there are single incidents—and these comprise the great majority of motifs." Thus, motifs can be persons or objects or incidents.

Alan Dundes (1962a) has criticized this system because its elementary units, the motifs, are neither quantitatively similar nor mutually exclusive. He suggested retention of the term "motif" and continuance of the motif-indexes as bibliographical aids but he also advocated introduction of the term "motifeme" and the use of new indexes based upon it as elementary unit. The word "motifeme" derives from combining Vladimir Propp's *Morphology of the Folktale* with Kenneth Pike's *Language in Relation to a Unified Theory of the Structure of Human Behavior*. Motifemes are the abstract and formal constants of a story type as distinct from the allomotifs which are the concrete and material variants which manifest them. Thus, for example, the three motifemes of certain treasure stories could be: Hiding, Seeking, Not Finding. Each motifeme could have a wide variety of allomotifs to fill out that abstract and formal sequence.

What is of great importance in this distinction of motifeme and allomotif is the hierarchically ordered levels of units and the strict necessity of comparing only units from the same narrative level. I shall use motifeme rather than motif henceforward to underline the fact that most of the time I shall be concerned with the abstract and formal constants of treasure tales rather than with the concrete and material variants themselves. Dundes (98) has claimed that, "The very heart of the matter of the folktale analysis is to ascertain what is constant and what is variable." This would mean that the mapping of the major plot options in hidden treasure stories will have to do with these constants much more than with their variants although of course there is no way to the former except through and in the latter. I therefore propose to rewrite Thompson's main motif numbers into motifemes as follows.

His index and all those modelled on it give these subdivisions under N500–N599. Treasure trove:

N500. Treasure trove
N510. Where treasure is found
N530. Discovery of treasure
N550. Unearthing hidden treasure
N570. Guardian of treasure
N590. Miscellaneous motifs

The first and last divisions are obvious catch-all categories but the four others evince the diversity of motif content which was noted before. These motifs include places (N510), incidents (N530, N550), and actors (N570).

I shall rephrase these divergent motifs into motifemes using the gerund for all of them: (1) Hiding; (2) Seeking; (3) Finding; (4) Obtaining; (5) Securing; (6) Using. These six successive motifemes form the canonical (or basic) motifemic sequence of treasure stories although, of course, any given story may well use only certain ones from among them.

The next stage of the investigation will involve examining each of these motifemes, along with its binary opposite, in the light of this general canonical sequence.

1.3 Hiding and Not Hiding

If one asks in what hiding places might treasure be concealed, the answer seems to be both anywhere and everywhere. But despite this vast array of possibilities, certain major distinctions and emphases are clearly visible.

1.31 *Places for Hiding*

A basic option is between treasure hidden *in cultural space* or *in natural space*. When treasure is secreted in cultural space it may occur either by historical accident or human design. From *historical accident*, therefore, the debris of ancient dwelling places, the ruins of abandoned cities, and the remnants of destroyed civilizations bear within their desolation treasures buried by the vagaries of war. Thus, for example, Roman settlements across Europe were the haunt of treasure seekers (Winter: 16) before they became the haunt of archeologists. From *human design* the possibilities are again somewhat staggering but I would draw attention to two major options. One may decide for *overt hiding* as in the Irish folktale (O'Sullivan: 240–42) whose chieftain protected three barrels of treasure from Cromwell's pillage by the simple expedient of pouring hot tallow on top of each so that, "When the tallow cooled down, you'd give your oath that it was three barrels of tallow that was in it." The treasure was then left out in the open and "Cromwell . . . didn't think the tallow of much account." Or, if one prefers a more *covert hiding*, there are all those secret places in attics and basements, or even a secret room within the house itself. So goes an English folktale from Oxfordshire (Parker, 1923:323) where "a hidden room was discovered there, which was evidently a priest's room, as it contained a prie-dieu. The man living in the house became suddenly rich, and began to buy property, so it was supposed that he had found 'a pot of money' in the hidden room."

As one moves from cultural to *natural space* as the location of hidden treasure, very interesting resonances start to occur in trove folktales. The fundamental option here is *under the water* or *under the earth*. Treasure found *under the water* has a quite normal explanation in folktales of the American Southwest where tales of hidden treasures and of lost mines have intertwined with one another. One Texas story tells how two rangers stopped to drink at a mountain stream and discovered on its bed "virgin gold . . . what miners know as 'drift gold,' which had been washed downstream from a mother lode . . . . miles away, but . . . exceedingly rich" (Littlejohn: 21–22). But water has a far more mysterious aura when it covers treasure in the ancient Icelandic sagas and Teutonic legends (Winter: 19). Here it is an alien element into which the brave alone may penetrate and from which the strong alone may return. In the saga of Grettir (Hight: 175–76), the hero dived beneath and behind a waterfall to a cave protected by its force, found and slew "a horrible great giant most fearful to behold," and, "it is not told how much treasure he found there, but there is supposed to have been some." The tale is obviously much more interested in martial prowess than in treasure trove but the water is an even more formidable ("very difficult") guardian than the giant. So also, from the other direction, when the hero must hide his treasure in Egil's saga (Jones: 239), three of four possible locations are all under water: "a great waterfall. . . . fens, big and notably deep. . . . hot springs . . . big holes in the earth."

1.32 *Superstitions in Hiding*

It is especially with Hiding *under the earth* that superstitious taboos and supernatural resonances begin to appear most clearly and this includes both burials in the ground and in hillside caves or mountain caverns. Obviously it is quite possible to conceal treasure *underground* for reasons of simple safety, be it *by* invaders in Ireland, where, "they say that when the Danes were in Ireland, they hid a lot of money in the earth, and only the *leiprechán* knows where it is" (O'Sullivan: 180), or *against* invaders in Norway, where, "during the Seven Years War, the Swedes invaded Trondheim county in 1564, and the farmers in the parishes buried in the ground what valuables they had" (Christiansen, 1964: 23).

There is a special situation, however, when treasure is buried with a dead person for use in the afterlife. In *The Heimskringla* (Sturleson: 1.223), the chronicle of the kings of Norway, a book described as "a waast wizzard all of whirlworlds" in James Joyce's *Finnegans Wake* (17:28), there appears the following law of Odin:

> He established by law that all dead men should be burned, and their property laid with them upon the pile, and the ashes be cast into the sea or buried in the earth. Thus, said he, every one will come to Valhalla, with the riches he had with him upon the pile; and he would also enjoy whatever he himself had buried in the earth.

Such graves, caverns, mounds, or barrows might seem fair game for treasure hunting but it also took courage or even foolhardiness to disturb this double burial of body and gold, this double return to the earth. On the one hand, there is the heroine Hervör (Tolkien: 13) who

> saw where out upon the island burned the fire of the barrows, and she went towards it without fear, though all the mounds were on her path. She made her way into these fires as if they were no more than mist, until she came to the barrow of the berserks.

On the other hand, Saxo Grammaticus records two barrow encroachments repulsed by supernatural agencies with disastrous results for the grave robbers. Harald found the burial mound of Balder (Elton-Powell: 1.191) and

> made a raid on it by night in the hope of finding money, but. . . . the hill split, and from its crest a sudden and mighty torrent of loud roaring waters seemed to burst; so that its flying mass, shooting furiously down, poured over the fields below, and enveloped whatsoever it struck upon.

But this "phantasmal" flood sent in anger by "the guardian gods of that spot" was not so terrible as what befell Asmund when he broke into the barrow of Aswid (Elton-Powell: 2.333) and climbed out again unrecognizable to his friends.

The listless night of the cavern, the darkness of the ancient den,
have taken all joy from my eyes and soul. The ghostly ground, the
crumbling barrow, and the heavy tide of filthy things have marred
the grace of my youthful countenance, and sapped my wonted pith
and force. Besides all this, I have fought with the dead, enduring the
heavy burden and grievous peril of the wrestle; Aswid rose again
and fell on me with rending nails, by hellish might renewing ghostly
warfare after he was ashes.

In the case of the Scandinavian stories treasure was "hidden" with
the buried dead primarily to enrich their hereafter. As such, of course,
the ghosts of the dead and the gods of the earth and the beyond would
be expected to protect such trove. There is also, however, a rather
horrible inversion or perversion of this belief in cases where treasure
is buried for concealment *and* a human being is murdered with it as its
ghostly guardian. Such stories are connected especially, and
appropriately, with seventeenth century pirate treasure trove and
such legendary figures as Edward Teach (Blackbeard) and William
(Captain) Kidd. These tales stretch from the Virgin Islands, where, "it
is believed that whenever treasure was to be buried the pirates cast
lots to see who would be killed to serve as a guard until the day of
Judgment when Gabriel would blow his horn" (Meade: 369), along
the Carolinas, where, "Blackbeard buried a treasure chest in the
marsh near [Pamlico Sound]. He killed and buried a man with the
treasure to guard it" (White: 1.692), and into "all six of the New
England states [which] received visits and conceal deposits made by
Kidd. . . . with which he always buried one of his men . . . to keep
guard over it" (Dorson, 1970:174). For those religiously inclined,
however, it might be better to emulate the story in which "some
Mexicans, wishing to protect buried gold, killed a priest and buried
him with it" (Von Blittersdorf: 102).
   No less superstitious, but considerably less murderous, are
Scottish beliefs (Henderson: 246–48) concerning the Brownie, "a
kind of half-spirit, half-man," who was "preferred as a guardian of
hidden treasure . . . in the earth. Some form of incantation was
practiced on the occasion . . . the dropping upon the treasure of
blood of a slaughtered animal, or burying the slain animal with it."
   It has been argued, and the above traditions seem to substantiate it,
that burial beliefs and treasure beliefs, be they religious or
superstitious, are very deeply interwoven with each other through

this common aspect of *under the earth* or *in the ground* (Hirschberg: 3). But we shall see later, in the section on Obtaining (§1.63), that there is an even more fundamental reason why taboos and superstitions cluster most profusely and cling most tenaciously around treasure *in the ground* or *under the earth*, apart completely from any association with the buried dead and their graves.

1.33 *Not Hiding*

Recall the well-known Aesopic story about "The Farmer and His Sons":

> A farmer, who was about to die and wanted to familiarize his sons with his farm, called them to him and said, 'Boys, a treasure is buried in one of my vineyards.' After he died, they took plows and mattocks and dug up their whole farm. They didn't find the treasure but the vineyards repaid them with a much increased crop.
>
> Perry, 1952:338, No. 42; Daly: 111, 271

This story is also found in India although here the moral is spelled out by the sons:

> Our father must have told us that his treasure was buried in the field simply in order that we should labour hard in it, and accordingly we have reaped the fruit.
>
> Grierson: 7.75

There is also a variation of this story known in Ireland which comes very close to a satire of its industrious virtue. A treasure-seeking peasant was advised by a supercilious (English?) onlooker in 1814:

> instead of searching for gold, to clear and manure the ground, as under this treatment it would yield results as if the crock of gold for which they were searching had been discovered. The strange part of the story is that this man, taking him at his word, rented the farm, and suddenly became rich; subsequently he gave his adviser a circular piece of gold, artistically ornamented, evidently of great antiquity.
>
> Wood-Martin: 1.188–89

In these versions all goes well and eventually they "find" the "treasure." But in another Indian version concerned with a wily Brahmin and some would-be robbers he manages to have them dig up *his* rice-field and empty an irrigation tank over it in a vain attempt to "find" his "treasure" (Bradley-Birt: 45–48).

Whether this story ends happily with the sons "finding" or unhappily with the robbers "not finding," something very significant has been glimpsed behind both variations. If the initial motifeme of a canonical motifemic sequence is absent, one usually expects the story to terminate before ever getting underway. But in the case of treasure trove tales it is quite possible to begin with a negation, an absence, a motifeme of Not Hiding. Obviously the motifemic sequence will not proceed in this case beyond the second one of Seeking. But this possibility of an inaugural Not Hiding introduces a basic instability, an unnerving uncertainty into the entire theme of hidden treasure. What if the treasure is not and was not ever here, there, or anywhere at all? What if one searched forever for what never existed?

1.4 Seeking and Not Seeking

> Those who have buried treasure have always seen to it that it should be hard to find, but there do exist ways of discovering it, though these methods are hard to learn and usually even harder to carry out.
>
> Thompson, 1951:262

1.41 *Superstitions in Seeking*

Methods and techniques for successful Seeking can range from the natural (maps, metal detectors) though the ghostly and the spiritual, the preternatural and the supernatural, and in some cases the exact dividing lines between these categories may be blurred or controversial. One person's belief is another's superstition and taboo to one is faith for another.

If one sets out deliberately to find hidden treasure, one may abandon the rationalistic world of maps and metal detectors and opt instead for magical helpers and supernatural assistants. These may be *objects* or *animals* or *persons* and their correct usage holds as many superstitions as does their existence and their location.

Among magical *objects* useful for Seeking treasure, the divining rod holds pride of place and the following description of its construction is surely a classic, even if one must wish the author better luck in his Seeking than in his Spelling.

A Method To Tak Up Hid Treasure (viz).

Tak Nine Steel Rods about ten or twelve Inches in Length Sharp or Piked to Perce in to the Erth, and let them be Besmeared with fresh blood from a hen mixed with hogdung. Then mak two Surkels Round the hid Treasure one of Sd Surkels a Little Larger in surcumference than the hid Treasure lays in the Erth the other Surkel Sum Larger still, and as the hid treasure is wont to move to North or South East or west Place your Rods as is Discribed on the other sid of this leaf.

Dorson, 1970:180

There is also a more grisly object suggested in an Indian tale (Tawney-Penzer: 3.133) about "a certain Brahman . . . who made it his business to exhume treasures . . . with a candle made of human fat in his hand . . . [which] fell from his grasp. By that sign he knew that treasure was concealed there."

Paradigmatic for all supernatural *animals* useful for treasure Seeking is the "tide mouse" of Icelandic tradition, a being which must be captured, kept, cared for, and returned with precise and meticulous taboos (Simpson, 1972:169). If these are properly observed the creature will deliver up "every day one coin of the same value as that first laid under it" from its "treasure lying on the sea-bottom."

Finally, there are supernatural *persons* capable of help in Seeking treasure. From Old and New England, for example, one could use witches and warlocks who work in conjunction with the other world. So, in 1611, "one William Bate had King James's pardon, and the record states that he was 'indicted twenty years since for practising of invocation of spirits for finding treasure.' The ground for this long-deferred grace was that the evidence was 'found weak'" (Kittredge: 89–90). Earlier, and more ghoulishly, there was "the trial of two treasure-digging sorcerers in 1465: they had promised their demon 'the body of a Christian person,' but they cheated him by offering up a cock which they had baptized by a Christian name" (94). And, be it clericalism or anticlericalism, there is the French superstition that a certain treasure can only be found by one who murders a priest since the "soul of the priest then becomes the necessary revealer" (Van Gennep: 418).

1.42 *Not Seeking*

I noted earlier the paradoxical relationship between the first two motifemes, the fact that just as there can be Hiding followed by Not Seeking so also, and more strangely, there can be Not Hiding followed by Seeking (§1.33). A second paradox now begins to appear but this time it is between the second and third motifemes. This will be discussed more fully later on (§1.54) but for now I would underline only the features of chance, accident, or luck, fate, destiny, or providence whereby Not Seeking leads to Finding.

Many examples of this motifemic sequence (by far the more usual one?) will be seen throughout this study but at the moment I am only concerned with those cases where the motifemic sequence of Hiding, Not Seeking, Finding is expressly underlined. Those instances where it is present but the emphasis rests elsewhere, for example with Finding accidents, will be left aside for now.

Imagine the situation of a man who is not only Not Seeking hidden treasure but whose indigence has led him to ultimate despair. Planning *suicide* is consummate Not Seeking. There is, however, a widely travelled story known from both folklore and literary sources and in both Eastern and Western variations (Aarne-Thompson: #910D) which concludes this suicidal Not Seeking with a Finding. In an Indian version (Natesa Sastri: 508) there is a rather loose connection between suicide and treasure in that the impoverished man

> was on the point of attaching the other end of [the rope] to his neck to suspend himself, when a voice was heard checking him from his rash act. "Desist from your mad resolution. Dig at the root of this tree, you will find seven pots of gold."

An Italian version (Parker, 1914:2.17), more plausibly and economically, has a penurious gambler preparing to hang himself and

> it was the will of heaven that the beam, which was eaten away and rotten, should break in two at the jerk he gave it, so that, still living, he fell and . . . from the broken beam poured chains, necklaces and rings of gold which had been hidden there in the holes made by the worms, and above, a Cordova purse full of crowns.

The Spanish tale of "Ramon the Discontented" (Busk: 131–39) beats this theme somewhat to death by having Ramon do it twice: first he hangs himself and "a stream of golden coins came running through the broken end of the hollowed beam" (133–34); later, having wasted all this first treasure, he decides to "dig a deep hole in the ground, and thrust himself in head foremost, and stifle himself that way" but, in digging the hole, he brings "to light a large jar heavy enough to be full of gold; and so it proved." There are also many versions of this tale where a dying father had commanded the son to hang himself only from a certain beam or in a certain place (Clouston, 1887:2.53–64). But in all cases, be it by random chance, paternal plan, or divine providence, the suicidal Not Seeking eventuates not in suicide but in Finding.

The would-be *suicide* is one example of a hopeless Not Seeking which ends up, by luck or providence, in a treasure Finding. Another example is the case of the *fool* or *numskull* who likewise ends up with a treasure despite acting in a way which caricatures luck or providence.

> The incident of a simpleton selling something to an inanimate object and discovering a hidden treasure occurs, in different forms, in the folk-tales of Asiatic as well as European countries.
>
> Clouston, 1888:146

Thus "a half-witted fellow, living near Baghdad in former times, sold his only cow to a chattering bird and when it "flew from its nest in the tree and alighted on a heap of ruins at some little distance . . . he accordingly dug, and found a copper vessel full of coin" (147–49).

And to this caricature of luck can be added the following travesty of providence which is also a well-known tale-type (Aarne-Thompson: #1643). I cite it in the Babrian text of Aesop

> A craftsman had a wooden image of Hermes. Every day he poured libations to it and offered sacrifice, but he continued to fare badly in his business none the less. In a fit of anger with the god he picked up the image by the leg and dashed it to the ground; and from its broken head there poured forth gold.
>
> Perry, 1965:154–55

None of these stories is particularly helpful for Seeking treasure. Instead, they canonize Not Seeking by suggesting suicide, stupidity, and sacrilege as excellent preparations for the fortuitous discovery of treasure trove.

1.5 Finding and Not Finding

The motifemes of Seeking or Not Seeking and Finding or Not Finding are, of course, close correlatives so that many points of the preceding section reappear in this one. For example, the connection of Not Seeking with Finding is seen again here in terms of Finding accidents, helpers, and superstitions. Also, accidents, helpers, and superstitions tend to merge and intertwine with each other and my present divisions are primarily a question of emphasis.

1.51 *Accidents of Finding*

Finding, subsequent either to Seeking or Not Seeking but usually the latter, occurs frequently by accident. Under this term I include, once again, the entire span from luck to providence. Lucky Finding, for example in Indian stories, ranges from the most magically implausible to the most realistically possible. In a middle India story "four great earthen pots full of rupees" appear suddenly on the horns of the buffalos used by two "very poor" ploughmen (Elwin: 468), but a south India tale of an equally poor ploughman details how "the leg of the bullock sank into that pit. . . . he dug and when he looked, a big pot full of gold was there, piled in neatly" (Emeneau: 3/1.133).

Such Finding can also have a providential design behind it so that the treasure is a divine reward for moral virtue. In an ancient Irish story:

> Angal, king of Corca Tri, stepped out through the door of the rath, and his right foot stumbled, so that a stone fell from its place in the fort; and it was the stone that covered the mouth of the flue wherein were the three horns that were the best in all Ireland. . . . these horns were not found till the time of the saints and of Aed Oirdnide mac Neith. For a veil was spread over them by God, till he discovered them to the king of Corca Tri, by reason of his hospitable bounty.
>
> Gwynn: 187–88

In an Indian story of providential treasure (Cowell: 3.16) a Brahmin who had carefully tended "a big Judas-tree" is rewarded by the tree-sprite ("a pious deed can never fruitless prove") with a hidden treasure which is not only indicated to him but delivered to his house lest "thou wouldst be weary, if thou hadst to dig up the treasure and carry it away with thee."

1.52 *Helpers and Superstitions in Finding*

Helpers in Finding treasure range, as expected, from the normal and the natural to the abnormal, the preternatural, and the supernatural. And, as with Seeking superstitions, so here also lines of division may blur at times.

Finding helpers can be internal, like *dreams*, or external, such as *objects*, *animals*, or *persons*, and to these beliefs must be added superstitions concerning especially propitious *times*, *places*, and *conditions* for Finding treasure.

Dreams can lead one directly to treasure as in the Chinese story (Graham: 253) of the lazy and impoverished man who "was sleeping on a big slab of stone, and he had a dream. The big stone slab said to him, 'My master has come.' Next day he turned over the big stone slab and saw a large jar of silver under it. There were three big jars of gold." But such dreams must be handled with great care since dreams are as mysterious and superstitious a phenomenon as treasure itself. They may indeed stem from a benificent source such as the Indian goddess Durgā who told a pilgrim "in a dream: 'Rise up, my son; go to thy own city of Benares; there is an enormous Nyagrodha tree; by digging round its root thou wilt at once obtain a treasure" (Tawney-Penzer: 2.159). But dreams of treasure can also come from a malignant source as in a Gaelic story from the Isle of Skye where the dreamer "recognized in the figure the Enemy of Mankind, he refused to be tempted. Satan having been baulked in his desire, which was to get the man into his power, desisted from his efforts" (MacCulloch: 317). A rather strange development of this theme is found in Persian (Lorimer: 311–12) and Japanese (Dorson, 1975: 245–51) texts where another buys the treasure dream and succeeds in obtaining the dreamer's treasure for himself.

Chief among supernatural *objects* leading to hidden treasure is the "odic light" (Gregory: 344, n.2) which was mentioned earlier (§1.32) as hovering over the heroic barrows of the Icelandic sagas. This motif has travelled from Scandinavia where, for example, "Hvirvel Bakke is said to be quite full of gold, whence it is that on every Christmas eve it appears to be on fire" (Thorpe: 2.263), to "the little Mexican town of Dolores" located "along the Rio Grande near Laredo" (Yelvington: 10-12). Here "there was a miserly old man who kept his money buried in a hidden spot, and who died before he could dig it up and use it, or disclose its hiding place to someone else. Since then a strange light is supposed to be seen at times . . . such as a lantern carried by a man walking might make." Phantom ships, especially spectral pirate galleons, return for buried treasure both off the coast of Louisiana (Yelvington: 1-9) and of New England, with "sails spattered with blood and a row of villain countenances grinning over the bulwarks" (Skinner, 1903:285-86). And these somewhat more fascinating specters phase off into more prosaic and culinary treasure indicators in English country tales, as when "a pot jumps about in a house; they dig underneath and find money" (Powell: 75) or the door of "a great big oven . . . used ter come right off. . . . move quite a few yards. . . . if you dug under the spot where the door fell. . . . it'd be money as you'd find" (Rudkin: 213).

Ghostly *animals* assist in Finding treasure and these also range from the wild and the exotic, such as the tiger in Chinese tradition (Graham: 197), to the more prosaic and domestic dog in English (Hartland, n.d.:238-40) and American (Smiley: 367-68) folklore. In an African story (Frobenius: 223) the helper is simply "a great bird from heaven" who produces a treasure of pearls, but in an Indian tale (Parker, 1914:3.183-84) it is the more specific "crow" which furnishes the "jewelled ring." Moving across the entire world, beast helpers can be a boar "a-digging the ground . . . [for] a mass of gold" in Ireland (Stokes: 154), a gazelle who finds "a diamond exceedingly large and very bright" in Africa (Steere: 67), a dog recovering his master's stolen treasure in India (Knight, 1913:42-43), or a fox who produces "a vault . . . [with] more than a hundred strings of cash" in China (Werner: 381). Finally, a French folktale combines both birds and beasts and reptiles in having a snake, a crow, a cock, and a dog help a man to find and retain a hidden treasure (Massignon: 239-40).

Stories of revenants, of ghostly *persons* returning from the dead to indicate (their) hidden treasure and so obtain their final peace, are found across world folktales, from a dead Brahmin in India (Mukharji: 100-103) to a dead squire in Hungary (Dégh: 291-96, 350-51), or a dead farmer in Ireland (Simpson, 1972:120-22). But such stories are especially prevalent in British and American tradition. They roam across Ireland (Westropp, 1910:344–45), England (Partridge: 341), Scotland (Chambers: 60–63), and Wales (Sikes: 151–53). Thence, I presume, they have emigrated across the Atlantic to Canada (Suplee: 272–73) and to all the major regions of the United States—East (Skinner, 1896:1.104–12), Midwest (Neely-Spargo: 82–87), South (Roberts: 35–38), and West (Hankey: 166). Revenants, on both sides of the Atlantic, include men and women, but the American tradition has added in, with some ghoulish delight, a few dismembered corpses which arrive by pieces to deliver their treasure message (Fauset: 543–44). Besides preternatural revenants, of course, one also has as Finding helpers supernatural persons such as a divine "messenger" in India (Dracott: 21–22) or "an angel" in Ireland (Stokes: 154).

Finding hidden treasure is much easier at certain *times*, especially when such discoveries may be considered metaphors for the religious festival upon which they occur. Thus a great treasure was discovered in Arabia at the Nativity of Christ, according to Irish tradition (O'Grady-Flower: 2.516), and so also will certain treasures reveal themselves on Christmas Eve, in both English (Briggs-Tongue: 44–46) and Swiss (Jegerlehner, 1909:16,178; 1913:237,267) folklore. But in Bohemian tradition (Hartland, 1914:175–76) it "is a treasure vault, the door of which stands open for a short time every Palm Sunday."

Appropriate *places* for Finding treasure are such miraculous or sacred locations as the ground where the Irish St. Brendan "planted the staff which he had in his hand in the sod that was nearest to him in the name of God, and found a pound of refined gold in it" (Plummer: 2.84), or the three superimposed and cross-marked stones beneath which a Spanish story found a treasure of gold (Gayangos: 465). But possibly best of all would be to find that Roman statue, or its fabled descendents, whose outstretched finger indicated hidden treasure with the explicit instructions to "Dig Here" (Oesterley: 438).

Finally, there are special *conditions* or methods required for Finding treasure trove. Some of the conditions are quite possible as in an American tale where a murdered man's treasure disappears if any one of the finders is not physically whole or morally pure (Danielson: 28–30). But the major portion of such conditions are so implausible or impossible that their imposition renders any Finding most unlikely. Indeed, the impossibility of Finding is presumably their point. Among such conditions is the Finnish admonition to use a one-night old colt on one-night old ice (Aarne, 1920:45,#65), or the English rhyme from the South Downs of Sussex: "Who knows what Torbery would bear/ Would plough it with a golden share"(Simpson, 1973:207). And lest a golden plow be not sufficiently impossible, there is the condition given in a tradition which seems to have leaped from the Baltic States (Aarne, 1918:129,#65) to the American Carolinas (White: 1.694): treasure will be found by one who plows with a cock and harrows with a hen. These impossible conditions are developed through trickery or scurrility, especially in some Lithuanian folktales of the more earthy kind (Balys: 234,#3615,#3616,#3620). Finally, a more elegantly spiritual version of this particular theme is found in India where, for example, a religious ascetic sees a buried pot as full of gold while an ordinary person sees it as full of scorpions. One needs special eyes, as it were.

1.53 *Not Finding*

There is also, of course, Not Finding, and then one can never know for sure whether the initial motifeme was really Hiding or Not Hiding. But as noted earlier (§1.33), whether consequent on Hiding or Not Hiding, the motifemic combination of Seeking and Not Finding can be prolonged for the length of the seeker's life or the length of the teller's tale. The treasure is never found but neither does the story ever end.

There is one particular cultural aspect of this motifeme which needs some comment. When treasure tales are compared with one another against the background of two vastly different religio-economic traditions in North America certain very interesting results occur.

It has been convincingly argued (Hurley: 197), on the basis of "about 250 treasure stories" that:

> American buried treasure tales have three main characteristics. First, they are told as true stories. Brief and factual, they have a simple and comprehensible inner logic governing events, as well as credible description and detail marking the narration. Secondly, their plots have a simple two-part structure, with the treasure being accounted for (or hidden) in the initial section, followed by the search in the final part. In the third place, American treasure tales usually end with the treasure *not* being found.

In my terms, their motifemic sequence is: (Not?) Hiding, Seeking, Not Finding. One is inclined immediately to interpret this patterned regularity as a cultural conditioning which insists that the United States may be the land of opportunity but that such opportunity is not exploited wisely in seeking hidden treasure.

This intuition seems to be confirmed by the analysis of treasure tales, not against the background of the American industrial revolution and social mobility but against a peasant and static economy in parts of Mexico.

> In a static economy, economic morality is opposite that of the Protestant Ethic. The American-style Horatio Alger makes no sense in this setting. No amount of thrift and hard work and traditional occupations is seen to permit a person to improve his position, so hard work is not a virtue. Thievery excluded, luck is the only avenue of advancement. The Horatio Alger of static economies, therefore, is . . . personified by the gambler.
>
> Foster, 1964:44

Which means that the pattern for treasure tales in such a situation will have to be: Hiding, (Not?) Seeking, Finding.

1.54 *The Finding Paradox*

I already noted one paradox in the canonical motifemic sequence of treasure tales, that between Hiding and Seeking, that wherein an eternal Seeking follows upon an initial Not Hiding, just as an eternal Not Seeking upon an initial Hiding, but the former is far more interesting and unnerving than the latter (§1.33). Throughout this present Finding section, however, we have been steadily catching glimpses of a second double paradox, but now between Seeking and Finding. Stories have constantly fallen into two groups, two divergent motifemic sequences: (1) Hiding, Seeking, Not Finding; and (2) Hiding, Not Seeking, Finding. And the second sequence was much more prevalent. This dichotomy has already been noted.

> But since these accidental finds could not be anticipated, deliberate treasure hunting relied on special paraphernalia, divining rods and stones, to divulge the location of hidden riches. (Invariably, however, science failed where chance had succeeded.)
>
> Dorson, 1970:179

This may now be sharpened into the question: Are treasure tales telling us that there is an inverse relationship between Seeking and Finding? Are we being told that seekers do not find and that finders have not sought? The answer seems to be in the affirmative because this double paradox of Seeking leading to Not Finding and Not Seeking leading to Finding is thematically developed within specific folktales as well as being latent in the pattern of their global totality.

There is a standard pattern widespread in folklore whereby the first act of the story involves success and the second act, wherein another protagonist copies the actions of the former, results in failure. Usually one's sympathies are to be with the former rather than the latter protagonist as the story is combined with a poor/rich, virtuous/vicious, or wise/foolish dichotomy. When treasure is the theme of tales following this structural pattern, "A poor, presumably deserving, clever hero obtain[s] wealth, but a rich, undeserving, stupid villain is led by his greed to lose his wealth" (Dundes, 1962b:169). But it must also be noted that when such "unsuccessful repetition" tales have hidden treasure as their theme the successful Finding is consequent upon Not Seeking while the unsuccessful act of Not Finding follows upon deliberate and imitative Seeking patterned upon the preceding Not Seeking! It should also be noted that the unsuccessful imitation often results in serious deformation or even worse. Not Seeking results in Finding treasure, but Seeking results not only in Not Finding treasure but in Finding death.

Examples of such stories are found all across the world of folklore. In a French version, which has travelled to America (Carrière: 208–12), the orphaned Peter is cruelly blinded by his foster-father but he overhears the forest animals and learns where their magically curative fountain and their store of gold are hidden. Healed and enriched he returns to his foster-father who proceeds to imitate Peter's lucky fortune. Self-blinded, he listens to the forest animals but they, now on their guard, discover him and kill him. In the Indian Himalayas (Upreti: 10–11) a poor man succeeds in binding "a murderous ghost. . . . [who] said if they spared him he would show them five jars of gold coin buried in a certain place." An envious neighbor "sold his house and land to others and went away with his family to the spot haunted by the ghost" but, since they were not courageous enough, "the ghost, seeing them all timid and cowardly, killed them one by one." A Chinese variation (Graham: 281–82) has a good, younger son find "a lot of white silver in a crevice on the cliff," but when the evil, older brother tries to imitate his actions the result is that "the stones on the cliff loosened and rolled down and killed" him. Finally, in Japanese tradition (Ikeda: #480D, #1371) the "old man" finds treasure by varied good fortune but the imitative and jealous neighbor finds only trouble, although in this tradition his fate is not usually as lethal as in the preceding cases.

You will recognize that none of these stories explicitly and directly states that Not Seeking guarantees Finding and vice versa. Indeed, the paradox can hardly be stated at all lest Not Seeking become a new device, a new if negative technique, and a subtle if secret style of Seeking. Paradox and paralysis here seem to be correlatives. How does one establish Not Seeking?

1.6 Obtaining and Not Obtaining

> The finding of treasure is not sufficient to assure its complete enjoyment. Very frequently there is an effective guardian over the hoard . . . a dragon . . . some kind of demon, or a mysterious woman, or even a sleeping king. . . . Under such circumstances the unearthing of treasure has its perils, and must be done with due ceremony. . . . Particularly are there strict rules of conduct which must be observed during the process . . . there must be no talking, no looking around, no scolding of animals, and the greatest care against unlucky encounters and bad omens.
>
> Thompson, 1951:263

It might have been thought that Finding could be considered as success in treasure tales. But, most especially where Seeking has preceded Finding, one's troubles are far from over. Indeed, with this motifeme of Obtaining, they are only beginning. This motifeme refers to the preternatural and supernatural forces that resist the removal of treasure especially when it is hidden *in the earth*. And here most of the superstitions about Seeking or Finding helpers (objects, animals, or persons) seem to reappear again but now as Obtaining opponents!

1.61 *Opponents and Taboos in Obtaining*

Under this general heading I shall be considering two correlative aspects of the motifeme. First, there are beliefs that supernatural forces (opponents) protect hidden treasure from disturbance even after Finding. Second, there are beliefs that certain counter-actions or non-actions (taboos) can and must be taken to offset and defeat these forces and safely obtain the treasure.

Such beliefs are found widely dispersed across world folklore, as noted both by my opening citation from Stith Thompson and by the following from one hundred and fifty years ago: "It is ever thus that supernatural obstacles come in the way of these interesting discoveries" (Chambers: 63–64).

Some supernatural opponents are temporary and selective while others are permanent and absolute. I shall begin with a less absolute tradition in which a hidden treasure is protected from all *except* the one for whom it was providentially destined. The Indian King of Vatsa (Tawney-Penzer: 2.52) is informed by a guardian spirit that "this treasure, which I have so long guarded, belongs to thee, as having been buried by thy forefathers, therefore take possession of it." There is a grimmer version of this belief from the *Arabian Nights* in

> an account of a haunted house in Baghdad; any person who stayed during the night in it was found aead in the morning. This was the act of a Jinni (demon) who was guarding a treasure which was to be made over to a specified person only. He broke the necks of all others, but when the right man came he gave him the treasure.
>
> Parker, 1914:3.335

In most cases, however, there is no exception and the guardian force stands against *all* finders. These opponents against Obtaining, like the helpers seen earlier for Seeking and for Finding, can be objects, animals, or persons.

Chief among *objects* as guardians against Obtaining are "illusions of fire . . . [and] thunderstorms" (Simpson, 1972:183–84), for example, from a New Hampshire story where, "in the course of digging, shattering thunderbursts and liquid lightning frightened the rash hunters into headlong flight down the mountain" (Dorson, 1970:182), or, from a New York tale where the treasure rock turned into "a blazing furnace. A column of flame the size of the rock—blue flame—shot up twenty feet into the air. It was so hot, they couldn't get near it" (Webb: 19).

The human imagination has, predictably, explored the major

zoological options in detailing *animals* as ghostly or spiritual opponents of Obtaining. These can be birds or beasts or reptiles. In British tradition the *birds* are usually crows or ravens so that many an "old castle and ruined monastery there has its legend of a subterranean passage leading therefrom, which some one has penetrated to a certain distance till he came to an iron chest supposed to be full of gold, on which was perched a raven" (Henderson: 320). As examples I would offer the following two descriptions and let their divergent rhetoric speak for itself. From England (Gutch: 394): "There is a tradition of a subterraneous passage running from the Priory . . . and a ridiculous story that midway in this dismal pathway is a large chest of gold, guarded by a raven or a crow." But from Wales (Sikes: 389–90): "In a certain cavern in Glamorganshire . . . is said to be a chest of gold, watched over by two birds of gloomy plumage, in a darkness so profound that nothing can be seen but the fire of their sleepless eyes." Those, on the other hand, for whom terror is colored white, know of cases where

> the earth quaked to let . . . forth—a creature all in white, a figure like a swan, that 'flattered and flew,' and made such strange and hideous outcry that the delinquents, casting down their implements, hurried off . . . from the grasp of the evil thing which his unhallowed doings had evoked from the recesses of the earth, and whose rage no human power might avail to appease.
>
> Hardy: 2.202

Guardian *beasts* extend from household to barnyard to forest, from cat (Drake: 276) and dog (Abercromby: 313) to goat (Jegerlehner, 1909:17), sow (Dorson, 1970:174), or horse (Skinner, 1896:2.270), and then on to less domestic and therefore possibly less frightening beasts such as the Chinese tiger (Graham: 195).

Reptiles as guardian opponents include an Icelandic waterserpent (Simpson, 1972:102–3) and an Indian snake with twelve heads (Fürer-Haimendorf: 215), and these beings merge quite readily with the dragon, a creature which must be considered the supreme amalgam of all guardian animals, itself bird, beast, and reptile, at home with earth, air, fire, and water (Smith). The dragon's guardianship of buried treasure has circled the narrative globe, from India (Tawney-Penzer: 3.133), to Greece (Perry, 1952: 582–83), Norway (Thorpe: 2.31–32), Iceland (Loth, 1962:113; 1963: 141;

1964:26; 1965:89), America, either Texas, where it has "two heads" (Dobie: 35) or Hawaii (Dickey: 28–29), and China (Werner: 209).

Turning, finally, to *persons* as guardians of hidden treasure and opponents against Obtaining, we are returning to something seen earlier in discussing superstitions about Hiding (§1.32). Most ghosts who are treasure guardians were either slain to protect the treasure or died because of its existence in some other way. Apart from such cases, about which nothing more need be said here, there also appear as treasure guardians all the various orders of the spirit world, from demons in India (Parker, 1914:3.169–70), through goblins in Italy (Penzer: 1.68), to the "little people" in Ireland (Kennedy: 116–19).

With this vast array of supernatural forces organized against Obtaining, it becomes necessary for the finder to be protected with special powers to offset their attack. Hence there is a long list of taboos connected to unearthing the found treasure, a detailed inventory of things to be done and not done during the entire process of digging up the treasure. When you look at these taboos and try to understand the logic of their imposition, it seems to be this. You are invading the world of the abnormal, the strange, the alien, and the other, you must, therefore, become yourself abnormal, strange, alien, and other. Almost every taboo somewhere has another taboo elsewhere enjoining the exact opposite, yet each, in its own way, places the obtainer within the realm of the uncanny and the mysterious.

Take speech as an obvious example. Over against ordinary conversation both complete silence and loud prayer are unusual and special. Hence, in digging treasure, absolute silence is an "international" imperative (Christiansen, 1964:20), from Egypt (Legrain: 97) to England (Anonymous: 237) and from Scandinavia (Christiansen, 1958:215) to Indonesia (Hambruch: 192). But, on the other hand, loud prayer might be equally efficacious, so maybe one should "loudly read the Bible" (Skinner, 1896:2.270) during the entire digging process. What is important is "otherness" even where and if such opposites to normalcy seem quite trivial. "The box which lies in this last-mentioned passage can only be fetched away by a white horse, who must have his feet shod the wrong way about, and who must approach the box with his tail formost. The box must be tied to the horse's head and not fastened behind him" (Addy: 58). It would probably help even more if the horse had wings and barked.

Just as with Seeking and Finding supersitions seen before (§1.32; §1.41), so also with these Obtaining taboos, one senses that, besides commanding the abnormal, they also tend to enjoin the impossible. To achieve the impossible is, after all, to attain the abnormal. Presumably the taboo against looking behind one, known from Lot's wife and Orpheus' loss, reappears here for this reason. Who could not look around to make certain of one's safety from attack and opposition after successfully Finding and unearthing the treasure? You can only sympathize with the Norwegian treasure finder (Christiansen, 1964:23–24) who, having safely unearthed "a big cauldron filled with money and valuables," sat down to rest, looked around, but when he turned back to the cauldron it had disappeared forever. So also with most of these taboos for safe and secure Obtaining. They are either so small that one ignores them, so minute that one forgets them, or so difficult that one fails them. As a result one usually loses the treasure, if not one's wits or one's life as well.

1.62 *Not Obtaining*

When you look at these supernatural Obtaining duels across the world, it seems that folktales have broken down the process of (Not) Obtaining the treasure into successive steps or stages of sub-motifemes and then produced stories in which supernatural interference destroys the operation's success at each possible stage. Imagine such successive stages in Obtaining as: (1) Digging; (2) Striking; (3) Uncovering; (4) Lifting; (5) Touching; and (6) Taking. There are tales in which each sub-motifeme has been safely reached before the taboo was broken and/or the supernatural opponents attacked.

1.621 *Digging*

In an Icelandic story:

> as soon as the diggers had got fairly deep into it, it seemed to them as if Helgafell Church was all ablaze, and they ran to put the fire out. Later, preparations were made to dig into it a second time, and this time they thought that armed men came up out of the ground and threatened to kill them if they did not stop digging.
>
> Simpson, 1972:183

1.622 *Striking*

The moment when one's spade struck the treasure was especially dangerous. In an American version from North Carolina, the

> correct formula was to dig for it, and after you struck the iron ring in the top, no word was to be uttered until you had it out of the ground. They told that every time they struck the ring, someone would yell out, 'The Christ, the Christ,' and it would disappear.
>
> White: 1.693

1.623 *Uncovering*

Again in an American story, this time from Connecticut, the

> lid of an iron chest had been uncovered when the figure of a headless man came bounding out of the air, and the work was discontinued right then. The figure leaped into the pit that had been dug, and blue flames poured out of it. When the diggers returned, their spades and picks were gone and the ground was smooth.
>
> Skinner, 1896:2.268–69

1.624 *Lifting*

In Icelandic narrative (Simpson, 1972:184–85) the diggers had got as far as totally uncovering the chest and

> one of them got down under the chest and lifted it, while the other hauled on it by a rope tied to one of these rings. But as soon as the chest was raised, the ring broke away from the end, so that it crashed onto the man beneath, and he died at once.

1.625 *Touching*

All proceeded safely in a Chinese folktale (Eberhard: 15) until the treasure was uncovered. Then "he put in his hand to feel what was there, but to his horror felt nothing but ants."

1.626 *Taking*

Finally, there is one last and most difficult taboo. One must not take *all* the unearthed hoard. Thus in Swiss tradition one can only keep a third for oneself, the other two thirds must be given for alms and other pious purposes (Jegerlehner, 1913:78–80,91–93).

With the motifeme of Not Obtaining reached, the treasure story must terminate at least as far as forward momentum along the canonical motifemic sequence is concerned. It is, therefore, as if each sub-motifeme just mentioned allows the story to be prolonged until the very last moment before Not Obtaining is irrevocably established. Will this occur at digging or striking or uncovering or lifting or touching or taking or at some other penultimate moment when success will be aborted and the treasure if not also the treasure finder disappear forever?

1.63 *Obtaining from the Earth*

Why do taboos and superstitions appear in such great profusion around Hiding and Obtaining treasure hidden *in the ground* or *under the earth*? Taboos and superstitions surround each of the six motifemes but they multiply especially around Thompson's categories of "N550. Unearthing the treasure" and "N570. Guardian of treasure," or, in my terminology, around the motifeme of Obtaining. It is as if they mount to a crescendo from Hiding, Seeking, Finding, into Obtaining, and thence taper gradually down through Securing and into Using. Most of these concern *unearthing* as if there was something especially dangerous about digging up a hidden treasure as distinct from just Finding it out in the open. Why is Obtaining so peculiarly fraught with supernatural danger?

My own suggestion is that treasure of precious metals or precious stones was originally *mined* from the ground or hillside or cavern and thus torn from the earth and its guardian spirits in the first place. It has now been returned whence it was originally taken, the chthonic harmony has been restored. To unearth such treasure is now a second disturbance and an even more profound alienation. Therefore, taboos and superstitions abound.

I term that a suggestion because, like every deeply imbedded superstition, it is almost impossible to be certain of its main source or principal cause. The closest I have been able to get to "proof" for the hypothesis is cases where mines and *treasures* are brought explicitly together under the supernatural care and protection of the earth gods but I have not found cases where treasure taboos explicitly mention the return of hidden treasure to its original chthonic source.

Two examples:

> The Quechua in Peru believe that spirits of the mountains themselves possess and guard the treasure, and hence the treasure

quest takes on a very different character from a treasure hunt in the
United States.

Dorson, 1975:xxi

Thus,

> in the pre-Columbian belief system of the Andes, the earth is
> animate and sacred. . . . [and] Andean legends tell of the earth and
> mountains moving their mineral veins about at will, causing mines
> suddenly to dry up to punish the white man's greed, or showing
> deserving Indians where to find veins of ore or caches of hidden
> Inca treasure (519).

Similarly, in Malay folklore, *mining* is subject to as many taboos
and superstitions as is treasure digging elsewhere. "Gold is believed to
be under the care and in the gift of a *dewa*, or god, and its search is
therefore unhallowed, for the miners must conciliate the *dewa* by
prayers and offerings" (Skeat: 271).

My hypothesis is, therefore, that this *chthonic return* whereby
hidden treasure has reverted at last to the earth whence originally it
was mined may be the deepest source of superstitious taboos about
Obtaining, deeper even than the association with thefts and murders,
graves and burials.

1.7 Securing and Not Securing

The motifeme of Obtaining was especially concerned with the duel
of supernatural forces consequent upon Finding the hoard and
unleashed *during* its process of unearthing. I distinguish all that from
Securing and I refer this motifeme to the *human* and *natural* dangers
or opponents through which even after successful Obtaining the
treasure may yet be lost.

The two most obvious ways in which successful Obtaining may not
be continued into successful Securing are one's own *stupidity* and/or
another's *cupidity*.

Stupidity, however, begets a very ambiguous reaction in folklore,
since the fool is abnormal enough to invoke superstitious awe. We
saw already that the Not Seeking fool often discovers treasure where
wise Seeking has failed (§1.42). Indeed, there is a motif-number,
"N551.1. Only weak-minded person may unearth a treasure," where
the fool is abnormal enough to offset the supernatural forces against

Obtaining. So also with Securing. The treasure may be secured *by* stupidity or it may need to be secured *against* stupidity. Thus in an Indian story (Davidson-Phelps: 41–42) the mesmerized reiterations of a "very stupid man" convinced the thieves that flight was called for and "so the fool saved the treasure through his folly." Then, on the other hand, there is the well-known story of the treasure finder who fears the knowledge will be stupidly blurted out by someone to whom he has confided the news of the discovery. So, for example in a Greek version (Megas: 179–80), he tells his talkative wife about two patent absurdities as well as about the treasure he had discovered and when she announces all three pieces of information "the old man kept the treasure and no one ever believed his wife again."

But the story that may be considered paradigmatic for this motifeme of Securing is the tale-type about "The Treasure Finders who Murder One Another" (Aarne-Thompson: #763). Basically the tale concerns two treasure finders who secretly decide to murder each other, so the first kills the second and then eats what the first had poisoned. The tale is known all over the world and has become enshrined in English literature as Chaucer's "Pardoner's Tale." It is associated with the moral teachings of Gautama in Buddhist tradition (Chavannes: 1.386–87) and with those of Jesus in Islamic folktales (Basset: 3.181). It may have two, three, or even four treasure finders murdering one another (Knowles: 45–46) and it may be bread in Italy (Di Francia: 141) or wine in Korea (Chŏng: 186) that is poisoned. But it is always the same story and it has always the same moral. Securing the treasure from human opponents is almost as dangerous and as deadly as Obtaining it against supernatural guardians.

1.8 Using and Not Using

The final motifeme of Using may be discussed as summarily as the preceding one. There are, of course, many stories for which Using is the major interest to which the other motifemes are only preparatory and in most such cases the story moves immediately into a different theme which does not concern me here. I am only interested in Using considered as the ultimate unit in canonical motifemic sequence for treasure tales and not as the initial unit of some new and different thematic development.

Once again, and even here, taboos and superstitions begin to appear. "Even after the treasure has been successfully raised, it seldom brings the hoped-for joy. Like the Rheingold, it frequently carries with it a curse on all its possessors" (Thompson, 1951:263). Such supernatural *curses* may be considered the final victory of Hiding and the ultimate danger in Obtaining and they continue the aura of superstitious awe which has surrounded every single motifeme in treasure tradition.

The archetypal treasure curse is probably the "bane" in Icelandic and Germanic tradition. In the *Völsunga saga* (Magnússon-Morris) the bane follows the cursed treasure wherever it goes. When the dwarf Andvari is robbed of his treasure he "cried out, that that gold ring, yea, and all the gold withal, should be the bane of every man who should own it thereafter" (48). It is acquired by Hreidmar who is thereafter slain by his dragon-son Fafnir. Next it is the turn of the hero Sigurd who kills Fafnir thereby fulfilling the warning made to Hreidmar and Fafnir when they first acquired the baneful gold: "thou and thy son / Are naught fated to thrive, / The bane shall it be of you both" (48). Before he is killed Fafnir warns Sigurd in his turn that the "same gold which I have owned shall be thy bane too. . . . and the bane of every one soever who own it" (60,61). And so eventually Sigurd will be killed by Guttorm (111), by which time one begins to ponder a new etymology for banality.

The theme of the cursed treasure is also found on both sides of the Atlantic, from the western and southern coasts of Ireland to the eastern shores of America. A gold treasure was found in Clare in 1845, "But the finders in some cases believed it to be fairy gold, and the people of Newmarket-on-Fergus tell that those who got it, with one exception, did not profit by it; the one lucky exception did not find his prosperity permanent" (Westropp, 1912:208). And in Cork, in 1631, the use of "gold that has the curse of Spanish blood on it" leads only to death and destruction, and its owner, having lost his daughter and his castle, "tossed from his boat into the water the cowhide bag that weighed so heavily" (Driscoll: 290–304).

Across the Atlantic it is the same sad story:

> Did hunters never find hidden riches? It were better that treasure
> eluded searchers, for tainted gains brought a curse upon their
> possessors. A chain of calamities ensued from the accidental

discovery of pirates' gold on Norton's Point in Penobscot Bay.
Dorson, 1970:186

Within the treasure chest was "a parchment bearing the words, 'A
curse on the man who removes this chest, and upon the region. Let
him beware, misfortune will follow him to the end of his days.'" And
so it was, with details too long and lugubrious to repeat here, through
six successive disasters as the pirate gold passed from one doomed
owner to another. There is also a tale recorded from the Wampanoag
Indians on Cape Cod (Knight, 1925:134) about a Frenchman who
sold himself to the Devil for a pot of gold but who was so frightened
by his bargain that "he buried the pot of gold, and fled. The curse,
however, had already come upon him, and within thirty days he
died." Later, an Indian found it with a "pointed money-stick. . . . but
within thirty days that Indian died." I would note, in passing, that
native Amerindian tales of buried treasure seem non-existent
(Thompson, 1929).

Seeking is Not Finding, finding is Not Obtaining, Obtaining is Not
Securing, Securing is Not Using. What, then, does the *cumulative*
world treasure tradition tell you to do if you happen to have got the
treasure safely and securely into your possession? Answer: return it as
quickly as possible! The following Korean story (Dorson, 1975: 293–
95) may be taken as paradigmatic for the entire paradoxical process
of hidden treasure stories. A king had received a bowl which could
never be emptied of whatever was placed within it and also a golden
ruler by whose measurements the dead could be revived.

> When the king awoke the next morning he thought it over and
> concluded that if he kept the treasures too long, there would
> eventually be too many people in the world and they would all
> become very lazy. He decided to return the treasures.

1.9 Motifeme and Value

We know that the simplest sentence demands simultaneous and
integrated mental choice along two verbal axes which can be
imagined at right angles to each other. "This is writing" is different
from "Is this writing?" along the syntagmatic or successive axis of
word order. But it is also different from "That was talking" along the

paradigmatic axis of word selection. Proper communication requires agility on both axes simultaneously, just as proper navigation requires both longitude and latitude together (Jakobson).

I have already suggested a canonical motifemic sequence for treasure stories (§1.2). The term "sequence" applies to *(chrono)- logical* order and not, of course, to *narrative* order. For example, Hiding must precede Finding chronologically but Hiding can easily be told in flash-back after Finding in a given narrative development. Individual treasure stories selected among those motifemes with certain obvious constraints and certain definite freedoms. But in any given story, in any syntagmatic presentation of treasure motifemes, there had to be something else at work besides the motifemic sequence itself. There had to be the reason why that particular syntagm was chosen and not another one. In other words, above every treasure tale, as above all human communication, there hovers a cloud of unsaying, a paradigm of unused possibilities, another tale that was not told, a different story that was not heard. I shall use the term *values* for whatever determined that the motifemic sequence chosen should be that precise one and no other (Saussure: 111–19). To create and to comprehend a treasure story one must have two elements: a choice of motifemes and a choice of values brought together in simultaneity.

Obviously a given teller or tale tradition may use only certain motifemes or values so that it is only from the synchronic vision of the total treasure tradition that one can determine either the *canonical motifemic sequence* or *canonical value hierarchy* and both must be kept open to continual revision as the tradition grows and our knowledge of it expands.

There were six motifemes in treasure tradition and they were related in a specific canonical syntagm, and there are also five values in a specific canonical hierarchy. I consider the values to be in a canonical hierarchy because the deeper ones can contain the less deep ones but not vice versa. Each of the five values, in the order to be presented, penetrates to a deeper layer of the human imagination although, of course, I am quite well aware that any such hierarchy of penetration is itself an act of the human imagination.

The first treasure value is CONTEST, the agonistic challenge implicit in the simple dualism of "hide and seek." This was already latent in the four major divisions of Thompson's N500s, leaving aside the initial and terminal catch-all classes (§1.2) as in *Figure 1*.

Figure 1.

N510. Where treasure is found

against

N530. Discovery of treasure

N550. Unearthing hidden treasure

N570. Guardian of treasure

Rephrased in terms of my six treasure motifemes this means that the initial Hiding militates against each and every one of the following five motifemes and thus creates the continuing tension which generates narrative development in treasure tales. Will Seeking become Finding become Obtaining become Securing become Using? Or will Hiding prevail somewhere along the motifemic sequence and the narrative immediately abort? This polemical tension renders every successive motifeme unstable and uncertain so that the CONTEST continues even to the very final motifeme, for might not a curse which had accompanied Hiding win in the end and, having destroyed the user, render Using impossible?

Many treasure narratives may never go beyond CONTEST as their dominant value but, if they do, the next two values must be considered as alternatives on the same level. One is not deeper than the other except, of course, by axiological decision. The second value is denoted by such words as accident, chance, or LUCK, and, its alternate option, the third value, is indicated by terms such as fate, destiny, or PROVIDENCE. I place them together on the same level because one person's LUCK may be another's PROVIDENCE. By LUCK I mean concepts of random chance, of being in the right place at the right time by pure chance. By PROVIDENCE I intend beliefs in moral and rational design controlling the affairs of earth from whatever transcendental source. The presence of these two values was already noted in Thompson's own classification. He had the class, "N. Chance and Fate" (Thompson, 1966: 5.74–138), and here, "In 'N' the large part that luck plays in narrative is shown. Tales of gambling, and of the favors and evil gifts of the goddess Fortuna appear here" (1966:1.21). Under this class is the category, "N400–N699. Lucky accidents" (1966: 5.105–35), and then the subcategory with which we have been concerned, "N500–N599. Treasure trove" (1966: 5.110–19).

The fourth and next deeper value is taboo or SUPERSTITION, the belief that there are guaranteed ways of controlling those preceding values of either LUCK or PROVIDENCE. By this term I mean beliefs that one must do this and/or not do that in order to prevail in one's treasure endeavor. Once again, I recognize the controversial possibilities where one person's weird superstition is another's sacred belief but I shall group under the rubric of SUPERSTITION all attempts to control and direct to one's own ends either LUCK or PROVIDENCE. Each and every one of the six treasure motifemes is surrounded by SUPERSTITION, from specific ways of Hiding which guarantee secrecy to specific ways of Using which ensure safety. I have already noted the profound chthonic implications of unearthing hidden treasure by taking out of the earth a second time that which was first mined from it and then returned to it. Northrop Frye (121) may well have touched on this aspect, quite in passing, while discussing romantic descents: "The buried treasure hoard guarded by a dragon, full of gold and jewels (which are of subterranean origin in any case), affords an obvious motive for the descent quest." There also seems more than normal moral disapproval behind Plato's famous injunction against digging up even unowned treasure. In *Laws,* 11.913 (Bury: 2.389-91) he says:

> As the first of such things let us mention treasure: that which a man has laid by in store for himself and his family (he not being one of my parents), I must never pray to the gods to find, nor, if I do find it, may I move it, nor may I ever tell of it to the soothsayers (so-called), who are certain to counsel me to take up what is laid down in the ground.

It is not just a matter of stealing another's treasure but of taking up

> a treasure which neither he himself nor any of his forefathers has deposited and thus breaks a law most fair . . . what penalty should such a man suffer? God knows what, at the hands of gods . . .

It has been noted (Hill: 3) that this

> extreme view of the sacredness of treasure is not paralleled, so far as I know, in any other writer. . . . that a masterless treasure, presumably concealed for the depositor's own purposes, should never be appropriated would seem absurd.

But Plato's absolute injunction against taking up what one had not put down, of exhuming what one had not buried, may have been sensing more a breach of cosmic harmony than of individual moral obligation. Even he himself was not immune to SUPERSTITION as he assures us that "men ought to believe the stories about these matters,—how that such conduct is injurious to the getting of children."

The fifth, final, and deepest value that I have discerned in treasure tradition is that of PARADOX. The other values could resound in any one or all of the six treasure motifemes. This fifth value, however, appears only in the tension between first and second or second and third of the six treasure motifemes. First, between Hiding and Seeking. Obviously, there can be Hiding without Seeking since few treasures are hidden to entertain searchers in the first place. But there can also be Seeking without Hiding, eternal seeking for what was never there in the first place. But, in these cases the narrative, however prolonged, must abort with either first or second motifeme. Second, and more important, there is a PARADOX between Seeking and Finding. Obviously, again, there can be Seeking without Finding (even when the treasure is really there), but so also can there be Finding without Seeking. Thus the motifeme of Seeking is the *only* element which can be completely absent and yet all the other five motifemes proceed without it in full narrative sequence. These two rather unnerving motifemic "non-connections" form a twin double PARADOX at the start of treasure stories and constitute the fifth value to be noted. One may find what was there but for which one had never sought, and one can also search forever for what was never there. In tabular format, then, the first three motifemes can furnish the plot combinations indicated in *Figure 2*.

Figure 2.

Initial Motifemes	Motifemic Combinations	
Hiding	Hiding	Not/Hiding
Seeking	Not Seeking	Seeking
Finding	Finding	Not Finding

That is, the value of PARADOX complicates very much the possible combinations of those opening motifemes. And this same complication shows up when the motifemes are placed in tree-diagram format, as in *Figure 3*.

Figure 3.

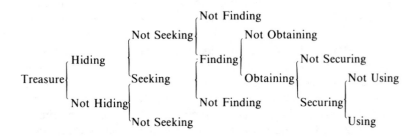

(You will recognize, of course, that the combination of Not Hiding and Seeking can only result in Not Finding.)

The motifemic axis and the value axis may be envisioned as moving along and across one another at right angles until, for a given tale, they lock in position so that the tale's meaning comes from both a selection of motifemes and a selection of value or values. This interplay, which is only visible when the treasure tradition is viewed synoptically and synchronically as a thematic whole, may be outlined as in *Figure 4.*

Figure 4.

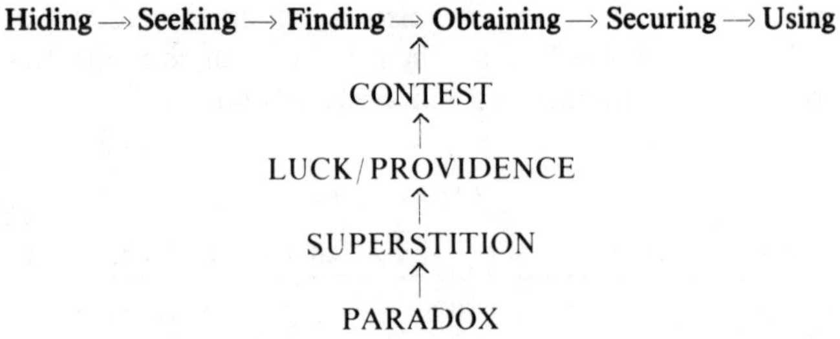

Hiding $\rightarrow$ Seeking $\rightarrow$ Finding $\rightarrow$ Obtaining $\rightarrow$ Securing $\rightarrow$ Using

$\uparrow$

CONTEST

$\uparrow$

LUCK/PROVIDENCE

$\uparrow$

SUPERSTITION

$\uparrow$

PARADOX

If, for example, a story believes that a hidden treasure has been bestowed on a finder in reward for piety (PROVIDENCE), there is not much room for the motifemes of Not Obtaining, Not Securing, or Not Using.

1.10 Play as Deep Value

Amos Wilder (140–41) has written as follows concerning one of Jesus' parables:

> In the case of the parable of the Sower I see two deep sounding-boards that lend power to the communication and which enter into its proper interpretation. These are like inflammable timber awaiting its fuse: the charged language. For one thing, man's relation to the earth and its processes is primordial and full of mystery. . . . A second sounding-board evoked in the parable goes even deeper. It relates to man's ultimate *conatus* or striving or going out from himself in search of fulfilment.

You will notice that he invokes both deep resonances and hierarchical levels within those depths themselves. What Wilder refers to as "deep sounding-boards" I am calling "values." I am not referring to them as "deep values" simply because, at least in some cases, they are overtly and explicitly manifested on the surface of the story itself.

There is, finally, one last question to be considered. The six motifemes were established only after a consideration of the worldwide treasure tradition. So also with the five values. But while those six motifemes could be present in an individual treasure story, all five values could not. My argument for their existence in the treasure tradition comes only from the entire process viewed synchronically. Hence the final problem. What is the *deep value* of these values, what is the meaning of their multiplicity, what is the parable of their plurality? I now use the term deep value because I refer to something that could only appear when all five values are seen and considered synoptically. It will resound in any one value only when it resounds through all of them taken together.

My suggestion for this deep value, this value of the values, this metavalue, in *PLAY*. That answer is somewhat predictable in the light of what I have written elsewhere (Crossan, 1976a, 1977), but I would like to offer a separate argument for it here.

In a very interesting book entitled *Man, Play, and Games*, Roger Caillois has suggested "a typology of play on the basis of which the characteristic games of a culture can be classified and its basic patterns better understood" (vii). His book establishes a fourfold typology of play, a fourfold classification of games (36,54): *agōn* (competition), *alea* (chance), *mimicry* (simulation), and *ilinx* (vertigo). My argument is that this typology of play corresponds quite exactly to the typology of value visible in the treasure tradition seen as a whole. In tabular format the correspondences are given as in *Figure 5*.

Figure 5.

Typology of Play in *Man*, *Play*, and *Games*	Typology of Values in Treasure Tradition
agōn (competition)	CONTEST
alea (chance)	LUCK/PROVIDENCE
mimicry (simulation)	SUPERSTITION
ilinx (vertigo)	PARADOX

First, *agōn* or competition. The correspondence requires little comment since competition or CONTEST adequately names the agonistic clash between "hide" and "seek." Second, *alea* or chance. I have correlated the values of LUCK and PROVIDENCE with this single classification of Caillois. He uses the term *alea* for "all games that are based on a decision independent of the player, an outcome over which he has no control, and in which winning is the result of fate rather than triumphing over an adversary. More properly, destiny is the sole artisan of victory, and where there is rivalry, what is meant is that the winner has been more favored by fortune that the loser" (17). Note the words: fate, destiny, favored by fortune. This indicates how easy it is to slip from a rather harsh term such as sheer random chance to more anthropomorphic and providential terms such as fate, destiny, or fortune's favorite which hint at rational design or logical control behind the scenes.

Third, *mimicry* or simulation, with which I have correlated the value of SUPERSTITION. If one imagines another world of preternatural or supernatural forces at work in protecting hidden treasure, one invokes taboos which render oneself temporarily alien, strange, and other than one's normal self. In *mimicry*, says Caillois (19), "one can also escape himself and become another. . . . the subject makes believe or makes others believe that he is someone other than himself. He forgets, disguises, or temporarily sheds his personality in order to feign another." The taboos and superstitions of treasure tradition demand that hider and seeker enter another world and to do so safely they must mask their normal faces, cloak their natural bodies, and walk in ways appropriate for such an alien environment. To speak is natural, therefore nature must be disguised by absolute silence to mimic the world of the uncanny and the unnatural.

Fourth, *ilinx* or vertigo, which corresponds to my value of PARADOX. Caillois (23) includes here those games "which are based on the pursuit of vertigo and which consist of an attempt to momentarily destroy the stability of perception and inflict a kind of voluptuous panic upon an otherwise lucid mind. In all cases, it is a question of surrendering to a kind of spasm, seizure, or shock which destroys reality with sovereign brusqueness." *Ilinx* is "the Greek term for whirlpool, from which is also derived the Greek word for vertigo (*ilingos*)." I have correlated *ilinx* with PARADOX because mental vertigo seems to me to be the immediate effect of paradox, the immediate effect of thinking too long or looking too closely at the twin paradoxes which form the core of treasure tradition. The mind spins at the thought of Seeking forever where Not Hiding had preceded and it whirls around the injunction that the best or only way to Finding is resolute Not Seeking.

It is probably this deep value of *PLAY*, resounding through the five intermediate values of the treasure tradition, which has rendered tales of hidden treasure so universally popular across world folklore. Because, in the words of Emily Dickinson (3.691), "Blessed are they that play, for theirs is the kingdom of God."

II

FINDING:
JEWISH TREASURE STORIES

> Do not lay up for yourselves treasures on earth, where moth and
> rust consume and where thieves break in and steal, but lay up for
> yourselves treasures in heaven, where neither moth nor rust
> consumes and where thieves do not break in and steal. For where
> your treasure is, there will your heart be also.
>
> Matt 6:19–21

The next step is to map the major plot options of Jewish treasure
stories along the general outline just established for world treasure
tradition. I shall be especially interested here in what seems
particularly or especially Jewish and these stories will be considered
in much more specific detail than was possible for the vast corpus
involved in the preceding chapter.

2.1 Jewish Treasure Options

First, one is not exactly overwhelmed by the amount of hidden
treasure narratives in this tradition and a possible reason is given in
the epigraph for this chapter from one of its greatest teachers. Israel
looked for hidden treasure, but not beneath the earth nor under the
ground.

The following story may be taken as the master-paradigm for
Israel's treasure imagination:

> God showed him [Moses] the great treasure troves in which are
> stored up the various rewards for the pious and the just, explaining
> each separate one to him in detail: in this one were the rewards of
> those who give alms; in that one, of those who bring up orphans. In
> this way He showed him the destination of each one of the
> treasures, until at length they came to one of gigantic size. "For

whom is this treasure?" asked Moses, and God answered: "Out of
the treasures that I have shown thee I give rewards to those who
have deserved them by their deeds; but out of this treasure do I give
to those who are not deserving, for I am gracious to those also who
may lay no claim to my graciousness, and I am bountiful to those
also who are not deserving of My bounty."

Ginzberg: 3.134–35

Apart from these celestial treasures, these "joys of Paradise," there
are also earthly treasures and many of these have been historicized
into Israel's own story. Thus, for example, during the Exodus from
Egypt:

the sea cast up many jewels, pearls, and other treasures that had
belonged to the Egyptians, drowned in its waves, and Israel found it
hard to tear themselves away from the spot that brought them such
riches

Ginzberg: 3.37

But the dangers of the treasures of Egypt are well illustrated from the
fate of Korah, who dared to rebel against Moses in the wilderness.

When Joseph, during the lean years, through the sale of grain
amassed great treasures, he erected three great buildings . . . filled
with money and delivered them to Pharaoh, being too honest to
leave even five silver shekels of this money to his children. Korah
discovered one of these three treasures. On account of his wealth he
became proud, and his pride brought about his fall.

Ginzberg: 3.286

Finally, all the treasures of Israel's Temple were secreted in the earth
from Palestine to Mesopotamia and must remain hidden

until the advent of the Messiah, who will reveal all treasures. In his
time a stream will break forth from under the place of the Holy of
Holies, and flow through the lands to the Euphrates, and, as it
flows, it will uncover all the treasures buried in the earth.

Ginzberg: 4.321

Second, most Jewish treasure stories are parables, short didactic
narratives with strong moral implications. They usually have the
form which R. M. Johnston (1976:342) has noted for such stories: (1)
illustrand; (2) connection; (3) illustrative story; (4) connection; (5)

application of illustration to illustrand; (6) connection; (7) biblical citation(s). The illustrand may be a biblical verse to be explained and/or a moral problem to be solved but this overall format locates such illustrative stories within a well-defined context of normative tradition. Although I may not constantly refer to this point, the biblical and moral aspects of such stories must always be remembered in Jewish tradition.

2.2 Trove Tradition and Jewish Stories

In the preceding and present sections I am considering treasure tradition in the larger and later Jewish collections (Ginzberg; Bin Gorion; Noy, 1963). In the next section I shall be concerned with the earlier and more official collections in the Midrashic and Talmudic literature.

The five stories to be seen here reveal the standard characteristics of Jewish treasure tales just mentioned and this is especially evident where and when there are other international versions for detailed comparison.

2.21 *The Revelation*

This story concerns one, "Bulan, King of the Khazars" (Bin Gorion: 1.341–42). It is connected to biblical history by its opening lines which identify him as a grandson of Japheth, and by its closing lines where:

> he dedicated the money and with it he fashioned a tent and an Ark and a candelabrum and a table and altars and holy vessels by the Lord's mercy and the power of the Almighty. And they exist to this day and are safeguarded by the king.

The story, using that term loosely, details how Bulan "was a wise man that feared the Lord, trusting Him with all his heart," how he purified his land and converted all its inhabitants to the one, true God, and how God said to him eventually:

> I have prepared two treasuries for you, one full of silver and one full of gold, so take them. I shall be with you and shall preserve you and aid you and you shall bring all the money in peace and build a house in My Name.

The sequence is not so much a story as a royal ideal, born of the Deuteronomist and the Chronicler, but located along the banks of the Don rather than on those of the Jordan.

2.22 *The Father's Will*

This is a slightly better story and also very close to a caricature of the connection between the biblical text and its illustrative narrative.

> A certain man used to teach his son every day the words of Ecclesiastes (11:1): "Cast your bread upon the waters, for you shall find it after many days." In due course the man died, and the young man remembered his father's words. He used to take bread every day and fling it into the sea.
>
> Bin Gorion: 3.1280–82

The story rambles around a little but eventually the son captures a young raven and its parent is forced to bribe him for its release.

> "Rise and dig down where you are standing, and you will find the treasures of Solomon, king of Israel." He let the raven go at once and dug down and found the treasures of Solomon, with many jewels and pearls, so that he and his sons after him remained wealthy. It was of him that Ben Sira said: "Offer your bread and your table and give to whoever may come."

There is an even more amusing application of the scriptures told during the story's early (non)development. A fish which has been eating too well from the bread cast on the waters, starts to eat his fellow fishes and then justifies this activity to Leviathan with this:

> Because they come to me and I consume them; and the words of the Prophet Isaiah (58:7) apply to them: "And do not disregard your own flesh."

It is clear from both these stories, however, that the teller is much more interested in treasures of wisdom hidden in the biblical texts than in treasures of gold hidden in the earth.

2.23 *The Mountain of the Sun*

This is a Jewish version of a well-known international tale-type (Noy, 1963:53–56). I had to discuss its structure of "unsuccessful

repetition" at an earlier point (§1.54). I noted there that the story's
dichotomy of successful Finding followed by unsuccessful imitation
was usually combined with other dualisms such as wise/stupid,
generous/greedy, virtuous/vicious, poor/rich, etc. Hence the Jewish
version does not create the moral sanctions implicit in the story's
dualisms. At the very most it heightens them a little. This can be seen
in comparing its opening lines with a Chinese version (Graham: 281–
82) which also concerns two brothers.

Jewish Version	Chinese Version
Once there were two brothers.	The father had died. There was only the mother and two sons. . . .
The elder brother was a miser. A stingy envious man was he, always chasing after money. All his life he yearned to gain the whole of his father's possessions.	Because the heart of the older brother was not good, he did not give any of the things in their home to the younger brother, but only sent the blind mother to live with him.
His younger brother was different. He was a good honest man, upright in his ways, and very fond of his brother.	The younger brother was very poor.

The story then unfolds in the usual way with the younger son assisted
by a raven in finding the treasure, "nuggets of gold, diamonds, and
precious stones . . . lying on the ground, shining and sparkling to
dazzle the eyes" on the Mountain of the Sun. He obeys the raven's
injunction not to stay too long on the mountain. "He filled his little
bag with gold, diamonds, and precious stones, thanked the raven,
and then set off for his mountain dwelling." The greedy elder brother
copies all his actions but he ignores the raven's warning not to stay
too long on the mountain.

> The elder brother did not listen. He wanted to fill his huge sack to
> the very top. He stretched himself on the ground and continued to
> collect more and more treasures. At last the sun rose with its
> burning rays and scorched the elder brother so that he was turned
> into a pile of ashes.

And in this instance the raven, not the Bible, gets the last word. "The raven fluttered his wings and called out, 'This is the end of a man who desired to take everything for himself.'"

2.24 The Inheritance of the Wicked

This is a Jewish version of another internationally known tale, "The Treasure Finders who Murder One Another," also seen earlier, as the paradigmatic tale for Not Securing (§1.7). But the Jewish version makes two very interesting changes which heighten (in so far as that is necessary) the moral of the story (Bin Gorion: 3.1317–18).

First, although there can be two, three, or even four robbers involved in different versions of the story elsewhere, the Jewish version has three protagonists who are divided into "a certain merchant of untold wealth" and "two deceitful companions." The two would-be robbers plot to "go and strike up friendship with him and find some clear way of deceiving him and winning his heart and taking all his wealth." Second,

> they took vessels of silver and gold, turquoise, sapphires, and diamonds and went to the merchant's tent and greeted him in peace. They struck up friendship and entrusted their money to him, they ate and drank together and then each one set out about his own affairs.

The story then proceeds as usual with each of the two plotters intending to poison first his companion and then their new friend. The plotters kill one another while

> the merchant in his piety and good faith and sense of friendship waited for them until he could delay no longer. So he went out in search of them and found them both dead in some entryway or alley. . . . their evil intention had fallen upon their own heads, while the merchant was saved and was left with all their belongings and property.

Two comments on the changes in the Jewish version as compared with the general story elsewhere. The division of protagonists into one virtuous and two vicious ones, as well as the latter's (rather implausible?) giving of their possessions to the former, allow a double moral to the story. The evil ones lose their treasures and their lives while the good merchant ends up both alive and enriched with their goods. But in the process moral value and narrative value are straining slightly against one another.

2.25 *Who is Blessed with the Realm, Riches, and Honor?*

My final example is a Jewish version of what might be termed the "King Lear" theme, the truthful but unacceptable answer of a younger daughter compared with the untruthful but more acceptable answers of her elder sisters, and I shall compare the Jewish (Noy, 1963:157-61) with an Indian version (Dracott: 20-30).

The Jewish story concerns a sultan with three daughters, the Indian one a Rajah with six daughters. It is the youngest girl whose answer displeases her father and who is then driven out of the palace only to be saved, in both cases, by finding hidden treasure.

But it is the royal and paternal question which is interestingly different in each story.

Jewish Version	Indian Version
In the morning the sultan would call out to his eldest daughter, "Who is blessed with the realm, riches, and honor, my daughter?"	One day he called them to him, and asked each in turn whether she was satisfied with her lot in life and what fate had given to her.
"You, father," the eldest daughter would reply. Then the sultan would call out to his second daughter and ask her, "Who is blessed with the realm, riches, and honor?" She would reply, "You, father."	Five of the daughters replied: "Father, our fate is in your hands: you feed and clothe us, and all that is to be provided for our future you will provide: we are well satisfied with our lot in life."
Then he would ask his youngest daughter, "Who is blessed with the realm, riches, and honor?" and she would always reply, "The Lord alone, my father." Each time the youngest daughter was given violent blows, but she never took her words back.	The youngest daughter alone kept silent and this vexed her father, who enquired why she made no reply. "My fate is in no one's hands," she said; "and whatever is to be, will be, whether so willed by my father or not." The Rajah was now angrier than before.

After the youngest daughter is saved by finding the treasure, the Indian story concludes when the restored Princess was "married

amid great feastings and rejoicings, and lived happily ever after. Such
is the power of fate." But the Jewish one concludes, "There was great
rejoicings in the palace, and before morning the girl's father
concluded, 'You were right, my daughter. The realm, riches, and
honor are the Almighty's alone.'"

2.3 Treasure Plots in Jewish Tradition

The conclusions from the preceding section are as obvious as they
were predictable. There are not very many Jewish tales of hidden
treasure in its standard earthly form and those that exist usually
evince the expected international motifs and types but adopted and
adapted to the moral and monotheistic vision of Judaism.

There is, however, one strand of Jewish treasure tradition which
will repay special attention. There are several reasons for this focus.
First, the strand is found in the earlier Midrashic and Talmudic
sources (Noy, 1954; Strack-Billerback: 1.674) but does not appear in
the larger but later collections of Jewish folktales considered in the
last section. Second, the tales involved in this strand of tradition can
be looked at synchronically as having a logical plot development as if
one story was trying to continue the plot beyond where another had
left it. Third, this sequence of stories seems to be far more
indigenously Jewish than any of the tales just seen in my preceding
units. Fourth, they are by far the most interesting Jewish stories with
which to compare Jesus' treasure parable and that, after all, is where I
am going.

2.31 *From Finding to Obtaining*

Looked at synchronically, these stories reveal three steps in a
sequential plot development. All of them have the motifemic
combination of Hiding, Not Seeking, and Finding. And all of them
are "complications" between Finding and Obtaining. But here, of
course, problems in Obtaining do not stem from taboos and
superstitions about the spirits of the earth but from spiritual respect
for divine law and the moral rights of human ownership. Indeed, it is
the introduction of the new sub-motifeme of Owning, with its
attendant ethical rights and duties backed by divine sanction, which
impedes the move from Finding to Obtaining. From here on I shall be

discussing both motifemes and sub-motifemes in these specific treasure stories.

The minimal tree-diagram necessary to furnish the plot options of these Jewish treasure parables is given in *Figure 6*.

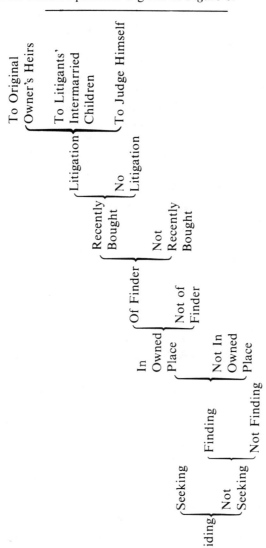

Figure 6.

Imagine, then, the following sequence of plot development across that diagram. In the first plot, the hidden treasure is discovered In Owned Place, Of Finder, Not Recently Bought. There are, therefore, no problems of ownership involved and it is the Finding itself that remains the center of interest. In the second plot, the treasure is found In Owned Place, Of Finder, but Recently Bought. The case is now a comparison between a seller and a buyer, a non-finder and a finder, and this contrast, and its meaning, may remain the center of interest. But there can also be a third plot if the seller (non-finder) and the buyer (finder) proceed to litigation against one another and, as we shall see, such litigation has a most surprising aspect in Jewish treasure tradition. But each one of these three plots involves moving a further step along the tree of options outlined in *Figure 6*. I shall now consider this plot progress in greater detail.

2.32 *Plot 1: Not Buying and Finding*

If the finder has not recently bought the place where he finds the treasure, there are no ownership complications but instead the meaning of Finding comes to the forefront and the values receive the focus of interest.

2.321 *Plot 1A: Finding and Providence*

There are three versions of this story, in the following places:
(1) *Jerusalem Talmud: Horayot*, 3.4(7) (Schwab: 6.276);
(2) *Midrash Rabbah*: Leviticus, 4.4 (Freedman-Simon: 4.66–67);
(3) *Midrash Rabbah*: Deuteronomy, 4.8 (Freedman-Simon: 6.97–98).

There are various small differences between the three accounts, but *y. Hor.* 3.4(7) and *Lev. Rab.* 4.4 are much closer to one another than to *Deut. Rab.* 4.8. For my present purpose I shall use this latter text and afterwards indicate one special variation found only in it. Here, then, is the story.

> Scripture says, *A man's gift maketh room for him, and bringeth him before great men* (Prov. XVIII, 16). What is the meaning of '*A man's gift maketh room for him*'? Once R. Eliezer and R. Joshua went out on a mission to gather funds for a charitable cause. They came to the valley of Antiochia, where was a man, Abba Judan by name, who was in the habit of giving liberally to our Rabbis. This

Abba Judan was now poor, and catching sight of R. Eliezer and R. Joshua who had come to collect funds he hid himself from them and went into his house and remained indoors for a day or two, and did not go out into the street. His wife asked him: "Why have you not gone out for [the last] two days?" He replied: "The Rabbis have come to gather funds for those who labour in the Torah and I am not in position to give them anything, and I am therefore ashamed to go out into the street." Now his wife, who loved pious deeds, said to him: "We still have one field left, sell half of it and give it to them." He went and did so; he sold a half of the field for five gold pieces and gave them to the Rabbis, saying to them: "Pray for me." They prayed for him and blessed him, "May God fulfil your need," and they went away to collect funds in another place. This same Abba Judan then ploughed the remaining half of the field, and he found there a great treasure and he became even richer than he was ever before. On their return journey the Rabbis again passed through that place and they said to a man: "We adjure: put us in touch with Abba Judan." The man replied: "It is easier to approach the king than him." The Rabbis said to the man: "All that we wish is that he should not think that we passed through this place without sending greetings to him." Meanwhile Abba Judan learnt of their arrival and he called on the Rabbis and gave them one thousand gold pieces. He said to them: "Your prayer has borne fruit." They replied: "We too were aware of your good deeds and we placed your name at the head of the list of contributors." The Rabbis then applied to him the verse, '*A man's gift maketh room for him, and bringeth him before great men.*'

The concentric structure of this version brings the value of PROVIDENCE onto the very surface of the narrative. The major units of the story are arranged sequentially in a chiastic pattern: (a) Prov 18:16; (b) alms given ("five gold pieces") and prayer requested; (c) treasure discovered; (b') alms given ("one thousand gold pieces") and prayer recalled; (a') Prov 18:16. The entire story is carefully framed by the double citation from the book of Proverbs which places it under divine providence even before the story begins. Then the providential Finding of the hidden treasure is both an answer to the Rabbis' prayer and an appropriate reward for past and future almsgiving.

This correlation between human goodness and divine reward, between almsgiving and treasure finding is underlined in *Deut. Rab.*

4.8, by mentioning the second alms, the "one thousand gold pieces," which Abba Judan gave the Rabbis on their return. This element is totally absent from the other two sources but these both emphasize the providential Finding of the treasure by adding this (from *Lev. Rab.* 4.4):

> After some days he went to plough the half field he had retained; and as he was ploughing, his cow fell and its leg was broken. When he went down to lift it up, the Holy One, blessed be He, gave light to his eyes, and he found a treasure there.

But, in any case, the line from alms through prayer to treasure is very carefully controlled by bringing the value of PROVIDENCE onto the surface of the narrative.

This intensive heightening of the value of PROVIDENCE in the Jewish story may be underlined by comparing the rather muted presence of it in a Norwegian one (Christiansen, 1964:20–22). In this tale of "The Silver King" there was "a man in western Telemark who was so heavily in debt that he was in danger of losing his farm." As he walked along "wondering what would become of his wife and children" he met an old man to whom he offered some snuff and the stranger "emptied the whole box." Having told his sad tale to the old man he was invited in to his home for the night. "When the farmer set out the next morning, the old fellow filled his knapsack with silver and said he was to pay off the debt on his farm with it."

2.322 *Plot 1B: Finding and Paradox*

The value of PARADOX has also been brought to the surface in a Jewish story by Philo, a contemporary of Jesus. In his *Quod Deus Immutablilis Sit*, 20.91 (Colson-Whitaker: 3.56–57) he comments as follows:

> On the other hand, it is a common experience that things befall us of which we have not even dreamt, like the story of the husbandman who, digging his orchard to plant some fruit-trees, lighted on a treasure, and thus met with prosperity beyond his hopes. Thus the Practiser, when his father asked him in this manner of the source of his knowledge, "What is this that thou hast found so quickly, my son?" answered and said, "It is what the Lord God delivered before me" (Gen xxvii.20). For when God delivers to us the lore of His

eternal wisdom without our toil or labour we find in it suddenly and unexpectedly a treasure of perfect happiness. It often happens that those who seek with toil fail to find the object of their search, while others without thought and with the utmost ease find what had never crossed their minds.

You will notice that the story is again connected with biblical texts, both with Gen 27:20 above and, later, with Deut 6:10-11. The tale itself could hardly be much shorter but it still suffices for Philo to surface explicitly the value of PARADOX. Seeking results in Not Finding, and Not Seeking results in Finding. But Philo qualifies the paradoxical force of his story by saying it happens "often." It is not, apparently, always so. Nevertheless, the paradox applies both to earthly treasure and heavenly wisdom.

2.33 Plot 2: Buying and Finding

It is also possible to complicate that simple first plot into a second one. If the treasure is found In Owned Place and Of Finder but which the finder has Recently Bought from another, the motifemes of Not Finding and Finding are compounded with those of Selling and Buying, and what will happen now between the finder-buyer and the non-finder-seller? Since we are now dealing with two individuals the value of CONTEST (buyer vs. seller) is involved in this second plot but in a special way, different from the more usual hider vs. finder.

There are two different versions of this parable attributed to Rabbi Simeon ben Yohai, a third generation Tannaite from the period around 130-60 C.E. (Strack: 115):

  (1) *Midrash Rabbah*: Canticle of Canticles, 4.12.1 (Freedman-Simon: 9.219-20);
  (2) *Mekilta de-Rabbi Ishmael*: Exodus 14:5 (Lauterbach: 1.198).
Since these stories are both short but interestingly different I shall give both in parallel columns.

The Dunghill (*Cant. Rab.* 4.12.1)	The Distant Residence (*Mek.* Exod 14:5)
	Another Interpretation:
R. Simeon b. Yohai taught [The Egyptians were] like a man who	R. Simon the son of Yohai, giving a parable, says: To what can this be compared? To a man to whom

inherited a piece of ground
used as a dunghill
Being an indolent man,
he went and sold it for a trifling
sum.
The purchaser
began working and digging it up,
and he found a treasure there,

he began going about in public followed by a retinue of servants—all
out of the treasure he found in it.
When the seller saw it he was ready
to choke, and he exclaimed, "Alas,
what have I thrown away."
So when Israel were in Egypt . . .

there had fallen as an inheritance a
residence in a far off country

which he sold for a trifle.

The buyer, however,

went and discovered in it hidden
treasures and stores of silver and
gold, of precious stones and pearls.

The seller, seeing this, began to
choke with grief.

So also did the Egyptians . . .

The reactions to Not Finding (Selling) and Finding (Buying) in both stories are framed once again by biblical citations and are allegorically applied to the relations between Egypt and Israel at the Exodus (Exod 13:17; 14:15).

Apart from minor differences, such as the more detailed description of the treasure in "The Distant Residence" as against that for the Using of the treasure in "The Dunghill," there is an obvious moral point added to this latter version alone. Even in the story, the illustration as distinct from the illustrand, there is a providential punishment for indolence and an equally providential reward for industry (my italics above) given to seller and buyer respectively. The full motifemic contrast is between Not Working, Not Finding, Selling, on the one hand, and, Buying, Working, and Finding, on the other. Hence the values of (moral) CONTEST and divine PROVIDENCE are both invoked in this second plot.

Once again a comparison with another variation of this story's plot helps to emphasize the moral and providential aspects of the Jewish parable. In an American story from Texas (Sutherland: 89–91) a man was twice told in a dream to dig under the white rose in his small pasture for a hidden treasure.

Then we got busy, but, after digging down about two feet, I found a large rock and quit. The story got out and I became the butt of many jokes. A few months afterward my brother-in-law offered me a fancy price for the place and I quit farming. Later on in the year I noticed that the little pasture had been plowed—the only mark of improvement noticeable. About the same time I noticed my brother-in-law buying property, including a fine family carriage, sending his daughter to boarding school, and getting himself elected to the state legislature. Maybe there was something under the roses.

Here the CONTEST seems to be between stupidity and astuteness rather than indolence and industry.

2.34 *Plot 3: Buying and Finding and Litigating*

In the second plot the CONTEST was not developed very far. The plot simply terminates with the one consuming and the other fuming. The inevitable next step is to move to Litigation and this is what happens in the third plot.

At the end of that second plot one could easily imagine the seller bringing the buyer into court and claiming the discovered treasure as his own. In this third plot, however, the CONTEST is not between a seller who demands back the treasure and a buyer who refuses to give it up, but between two individuals of such superlative virtue and scrupulous conscience that each demands the other keep the discovered hoard. I shall be discussing different judgments on the Litigation but, in all cases, the suit is between a buyer who wishes to return the treasure and a seller who refuses to accept it.

2.341 *Plot 3A: Litigation and One Judgment*

A first example of this most pious Litigation, and an equally pious judgment, is given as illustration of the sincere repentance of Nineveh after the preaching of Jonah.

> One incident that happened at the time will illustrate the contrition of the Ninevites. A man found a treasure in the building lot he had acquired from his neighbor. Both buyer and seller refused to assume possession of the treasure. The seller insisted that the sale of the lot carried with it the sale of all it contained. The buyer held that he had bought the ground, not the treasure hidden therein. Neither rested satisfied until the judge succeeded in finding out who had

hidden the treasure and who were his heirs, and the joy of the two
was great when they could deliver the treasure up to its legitimate
owners.

Ginzberg: 4.251

Ginzberg (6.351, n.35) has commented that, "The narrative is a
variation of an Alexander legend, which has a great vogue in Jewish
literature." But it should be noted that, while the Litigation is the
same here as there, the *judgments* rendered in the Alexander legend,
to which I now turn, are both quite different from the option chosen
in the Nineveh version.

2.342 *Plot 3B: Litigation and Two Judgments*

There are, as Ginzberg noted, very many versions of this story in
the Talmudic-Midrashic literature, for example:
  (1) *Jerusalem Talmud: Baba Meṣi'a,* 2.5 (Schwab: 6.94);
  (2) *Midrash Rabbah*: Genesis, 33.1 (Freedman-Simon: 1.258–59);
  (3) *Midrash Rabbah:* Leviticus, 27.1 (Freedman-Simon: 4.342–
      43);
  (4) *Pesiḳta de-Rab Kahana,* 9.1 (Braude-Kapstein: 171–72);
  (5) *Midrash Tanḥuma*: Emor, 9 (Buber: 2.88–89).
Despite this number, however, the story remains remarkably the
same and I shall cite the Talmudic account in the translation of L.
Wallach (63–64):

> Alexander of Macedon visited King Kazia. The latter showed him
> much gold and silver. Alexander said to him: "I do not need your
> gold and silver. I came only because I wished to see your method
> . . . how you act and how you dispense justice." While he was
> arguing with him, a man came with a complaint against his
> neighbor who had sold him an unploughed field, and in digging it
> the buyer happened to find a treasure of denars [in a dunghill]. The
> buyer argued: I bought [the field and] the dunghill [in it], but I did
> not buy the treasure. The seller maintained: I sold [the field and] the
> dunghill and all it contained. . . . While both were discussing the
> problem, the king said to one of them, "Have you a son?" "Yes," he
> replied. Then he asked the other, "Have you a daughter?" "Yes," he
> said. Said the king to both: "Then marry them and let the treasure
> belong to both." Alexander laughed [at the king's decision] and the
> king asked him, "Why are you laughing? Have I not judged well?
> Had this happened among you [in your empire], how would you

have judged?" Alexander replied, "We should have killed both, and the treasure would have gone to the king."

The Jewish version of this piece of black humor gives the last word to the king. He asks Alexander if rain falls for the cattle in his country and then asserts that with such a ruler as Alexander this could be only by the mercy of God. He applies Ps 36:7(6), "Man and beast thou savest, O Lord," to the situation as God saves Alexander (man) only because of the cattle (beast) in his kingdom.

This story is deeply involved in the difficult problem of "the relations between the Talmudic Alexander traditions and the Alexander romance" (Wallach: 80) and Wallach (75) has argued that his "investigation has clearly established the Greek origin of the legend." Despite the fact that two words in the legend are hebraicized Greek, the Jewish origin of the story seems much more likely. It is better, therefore, to agree with Israel Lévi (1881a, 1881b, 1883) that the story "seems of Jewish origin . . . and, since no earlier source records the legend, one must suppose, pending proof to the contrary, that it is a product of Jewish imagination" (1883:84,85), and with Joseph Klausner (380) that, "It is noteworthy that this story of a Greek character is repeated throughout the Jewish *Midrashic* literature but is not found at all in Greek literature; it was not in accordance with the Greek spirit."

There is, however, an example of this plot type in Greek literature and it can serve as foil for the Jewish version. In *The Life of Apollonius of Tyana*, 2.39 (Conybeare: 1.218–21), Philostratus tells how the sage had travelled to India and King Phraotes asked his advice on a law-suit.

> I admit, [said the king], that I am perplexed; and that is why I want your advice; for one man has sold to another land, in which there lay a treasure as yet undiscovered, and some time afterwards the land, being broken up, revealed a certain chest, which the person who sold the land says belongs to him rather than to the other, for that he would never have sold the land, if he had known beforehand that he had a fortune thereon; but the purchaser claims that he acquired everything that he found in land, which henceforth was his. And both these contentions are just; and I shall seem ridiculous if I order them to share the gold between them, for any old woman could settle the matter in that way.

It is interesting to note that Apollonius' advice is, *mutatis mutandis*, based on the value of PROVIDENCE and is closer at this point to the Jewish second rather than third plot:

> It seems to me, O king, right to weigh these men in the balance, as it were, and to examine their respective lives; for I cannot believe that the gods would deprive the one even of his land, unless he had been a bad man, or that they would, on the other hand, bestow on the other even what was under the land, unless he had been better than the man who sold it." The two claimants came back the next day, and the seller was convicted of being a ruffian who had neglected the sacrifices to the gods on that land; but the other was found to be a decent man and a most devout worshipper of the gods. Accordingly, the opinion of Apollonius prevailed, and the better of the two men quitted the court as one on whom the gods had bestowed the boon.

Apart, however, from the judgment, the Litigation itself is the more expected human dispute in such a case, a suit to get rather than one to give up the treasure. Against this more expected Litigation, the Jewish third plot stands out as an instance of most scrupulous piety and most conscientious morality.

2.4 Values in Jewish Treasure Tradition

All the stories considered in this chapter have chosen the motifemic sequence of Hiding, Not Seeking, Finding, so there is little evidence of the value of CONTEST in the usual sense of Hiding militating against all the other motifemes, that is, of hide vs. seek. But CONTEST appears in these stories between Finding (the buyer) and Not Finding (the seller) in Plot 2, where the one's industry prevailed over the other's indolence, and in Plot 3, where the extraordinary virtue of both prevailed over normal human greed. In these cases CONTEST is already covered with a moral and providential mantle from the start.

The value of LUCK gives way, of course, completely to that of PROVIDENCE in this tradition. Consequent upon this emphasis, the value of SUPERSTITION, does not appear at all in any of the forms known in the general tradition. Since relations between God and the individual are regulated by sacred covenant and moral law in

Jewish stories, the only Obtaining difficulties, if there are any, must concern ownership so that LAW replaces totally the value of SUPERSTITION for the Jewish tradition. What one should or should not do is determined by LAW and there is no way to prevail against that divine power. Not taboo and superstition but covenant and law determine the Obtaining in Jewish treasure parables. This also means that the values of PROVIDENCE and LAW will combine very closely in these stories. Finally, there is the value of PARADOX. This is implicitly present in the very motifemic sequence chosen by these tales but only in the case of Philo's parable is this explicitly thematized as the double paradox of seekers not finding and finders not having sought. But although he does use this as an image for relations between God and the world he qualifies the PARADOX by saying that this happens "often." He does not say it happens always.

III

LOSS:
JESUS' TREASURE PARABLE

[Negative experience] teaches not solely by leading us to revise the
context of our subsequent experience so that the new fits into the
corrected unity of an objective interpretation. . . . Not only is the
object of the experience presented differently, but the experiencing
consciousness changes. The action of a negative experience is one of
becoming conscious of oneself. Whatever one becomes conscious
of are the motifs which have been guiding experience and which
have remained unquestioned in this guiding function. Negative
experience has primarily the character of self-experience, which
frees one for a qualitatively new kind of experience.
                                    G. Buck, in H. R. Jauss (33, n.77)

The third and final step in this experiment is to consider Jesus'
treasure parable against the general background of world treasure
folktales and the immediate background of his own Jewish treasure
tradition. It will conclude with an analysis of the parable's meaning
using a philosophy of language and of narrative hopefully adequate
to its paradoxical radicality.

3.1 Jesus' Parable and World Folklore

The only version of this parable now available is in Matt 13:44,
"The kingdom of heaven is like a treasure hidden in a field, which a
man found and covered up; then in his joy he goes and sells all that he
has and buys that field."

3.11 *Motifemes in Jesus' Parable*

The story breaks down into six narrative units, six motifemes or
sub-motifemes of the canonical treasure structure. For simplicity I

shall use the single term motifeme to refer to both smaller and larger units in the parable.

3.111 *Hiding in the Earth*

The treasure motifeme of Hiding in the Earth appears in Jesus' story through and in the phrase, "hidden in a field." Two effects are immediately produced. First, the tale starts down one of the widest and best travelled routes of treasure folklore. Its beginning is, in other words, about as obvious as it could be. Stith Thompson's index (1966:5.110–13), for example, devotes two and a half pages to "N510. Where treasure is found" and one full page is taken up by "N511. Treasure in ground." Second, the chthonic reverberations are immediately established and the value of SUPERSTITION is invoked from world folklore at least as a hovering possibility. I have already drawn repeated attention to this conjunction of treasure and superstition in world treasure tradition. Indeed, even if there were no treasure stories extant, this conjunction would be equally well known from the laws against it in ancient and medieval decrees and codes (Hill: 307, under "Magic").

3.112 *Not Seeking*

If the former motifeme was the most expected one in world treasure lore, the present one is almost absolutely predictable in Jewish stories. It is as if Jesus had started down a major road and then took a quite expected turn along a more local connection. The opening motifemic sequence is, therefore, Hiding, Not Seeking, Finding. Its motto might well be: Do not seek and you shall find.

3.113 *Finding in Another's Land*

There are two points to be made here. First, Jesus' story has suddenly taken a very significant turn. The motifeme of Finding in Another's Land makes Another stand out over Land, and chthonic reverberations recede before questions of ownership, problems either of morality or of guile. The value of CONTEST comes forcibly to the surface of the story and the conflict will be between right and wrong as well as between the finder and the owner of the land. And as the value of SUPERSTITION recedes so also will, in characteristically

Jewish fashion, the values of divine covenant and moral law come to
the forefront.

The plot option chosen by Jesus at this point may be underlined by
comparing it with a treasure story from the Roman world as recorded
both by Horace around 30 B.C.E. and Porphyrio of Tyre (232-304
C.E.). The contrast can be indicated by taking a section from the
earlier *Figure 6* and repeating it here as *Figure 7*. This diagram shows
that there were three options possible for Jesus' story at this
motifemic decision. The Finding could have been: (a) Not in Owned
Place; (b) In Owned Place, but of Finder; (c) In Owned Place, but Not
Of Finder.

Figure 7.

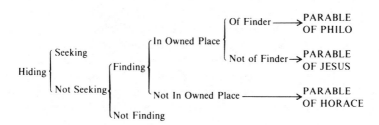

I have already discussed that second or (b) option in terms of Plots 1,
2, and 3 of the Jewish tradition (§2.3), for example, in Philo's parable
(§2.322). It only remains now to add some considerations of the first
or (a) option as exemplified by Horace's parable, in order to locate
Jesus' chosen parabolic plot against its most proximate plot
possibilities for this motifeme.

Satires, 2.6.1-15 (Fairclough: 210-11) opens with Horace
ensconced in bucolic beatitude on his Sabine farm. He assures
Mercury, god of gain, that he desires nothing more "save that thou
make these blessings last my life long." He guarantees Mercury that
he at least will never utter two such foolish prayers as these. First, he
will never ask to have his lands expanded just to make their shape
more pleasing to the eye. Second, he will never pray, "O that some
lucky strike would disclose to me a pot of money, like the man who,
having found a treasure-trove, bought and ploughed the self-same
ground he used to work on hire, enriched by favor of Hercules!"

Why exactly does Horace consider this second prayer to be foolish? It was not that the wishful dreaming of the prayer was itself stupid since, in the story, it was granted fulfilment. What renders the initial prayer useless is the stupidity of the servant whose imagination cannot absorb the implications of his new and god-given wealth. What Horace ironically contemplates and satirically castigates is the stupidity of one who continues to plow as owner what once he worked as servant. He never considers hiring and paying another to plow in his stead as *his* servant. His imagination is too weak for the actual transition from *mercennarius* to *mercatus*. Put proverbially, you can take the plower out of the field but you can't take the field out of the plower.

It must be noted, therefore, that Horace's story does not envisage the case where a servant *found a treasure while plowing in the field of his master and bought the field to obtain the treasure* as, presumably or possibly, is the case in Jesus' parable. Horace's text reads as follows: "O si urnam argenti fors quae mihi monstret, ut illi, thesauro invento qui mercennarius agrum illum ipsum mercatus aravit, dives amico Hercule!" The correct Loeb translation cited above may be compared with this Modern Library one (Kraemer: 71, my italics). "If only I could accidentally find a pot of gold, like the hireling who discovered the treasure and bought and ploughed in his own right the field *where he found it.* Hercules was a good friend to him!" Such a mistranslation, more reminiscent of Matthew's Greek than of Horace's Latin, loses quite totally the ironic point of Horace's parable and would have proved the servant's wily sagacity rather than his unchanged stupidity. This is especially true since "the Roman law was undecided whether a finder of treasure was or was not legally entitled to buy the field without revealing his knowledge that the treasure was there. The view which ultimately prevailed was that an owner who did not know of the existence of the treasure did not possess it, though he possessed the land" (Derrett: 2–3). But, for Horace, the story's supercilious and ironic moral claims that a peasant enriched is just an enriched peasant and the heart of the parable is the lack of change from the peasant worker to the peasant owner.

A longer version of this folktale is given by the Neoplatonic philosopher, Porphyrio of Tyre (Holder: 313; Morris: 222), and, while it takes him sixty-one words to do what the lean and economical lines of Horace did in thirteen, the satirical moral appears so much the more clearly thereby. Here is his version:

> The story is told about a certain laborer who continually implored Hercules to grant him some favor. Hercules obtained the assistance of Mercury and had him discover a hidden treasure-trove. The man dug it up, bought the field he usually labored in for pay, and proceeded to work there just like before. Thus Mercury was proved correct in what he had already told Hercules, that nothing could make such a man live at ease ("beatum vivere") since he continued to work then as always.

Horace, it can be noted, kept Mercury in the context but outside the story while retaining Hercules inside it, and he gave no hint that the story's moral had been foretold by Mercury to Hercules, as in the longer version of Porphyrio. But, in any case, the point of both versions is exactly the same and Horace must have known some account very similar to Porphyrio's in order to explain his combination of Mercury and Hercules in the context. The presence of the two gods does not change the story's moral but serves, more clearly and explicitly in Porphyrio than in Horace, to reiterate the ironic point.

Horace's parable was interested in stupidity rather than morality and to avoid any distraction from legal or ethical considerations he used or took the motifeme of Finding but Not In Owned Place. Jesus' parable, on the other hand, chose a very different option.

All the preceding is my first point concerning this motifeme in Jesus' story. The second point is that Jesus' *narration* of his plot holds this motifeme until the very end of the narrative, or, better, it places the motifeme of Finding in its normal canonical sequence but withholds the sub-motifeme of In Owned Place but Not of Finder until the very end of the narration. It is only when the verb "buys" is narrated that we know for sure and retrospectively that the Finding was in fact on another's land. I shall return to this feature of *plot narration* later in discussing Jesus' sixth motifeme (§3.116)

3.114 *Rehiding the Treasure*

I do not intend to suggest a stemma for all the alternative possibilities confronting Jesus' story after its third motifeme. Instead,

I shall stay very close to the motifemes chosen by him and will compare them with all the similar motifemes from world treasure tradition which I have managed to find. It would be both unwise and impertinent to claim that I have found all the parallels that exist but in these cases I am using *all* that I discovered.

One most obvious option for Jesus's fourth motifeme would be Telling or Not Telling. Will the finder tell the land's owner about the treasure and what will happen if he does? Will it be like the Italian folktale (Penzer: 1.68–69) about one Cienzo who was spending the night in another's cellar? Three goblins appear and tell him to "go and take this treasure which is destined for you alone." But Cienzo shouts until the master of the property comes down into the cellar:

> As soon as he reached the bottom he saw before him a great treasure of which he at once took possession, but not without offering Cienzo his proper share; Cienzo refused it, however, and taking his dog in his arms got on his horse and set out again on his journey.

Will Jesus' parable offer us a model of such high ethical ideal by having the finder shout immediately for the owner of the land?

Instead, we find the motifeme of Rehiding the Treasure, which is, at best, rather ambiguous. On the one hand, there is the Indian tale of Sattvaśila (Tawney-Penzer: 3.158–59) who found a treasure out of which "he provided himself with pleasures and gave wealth to Brāhmans, slaves and friends, and thus the virtuous man spent his life." But the king heard of his good fortune and

> Sattvaśila was summoned by the king, and by order of the doorkeeper remained standing for a moment in a lonely part of the king's courtyard. There, as he was scratching the earth . . . he found another large treasure in a copper vessel. It appeared like his own heart, displayed openly for him by Destiny, pleased with his virtue, in order that he might propitiate the king with it. *So he covered it up again with the earth as it was before*, and when summoned by the doorkeeper he entered the king's presence.

My italics note the Rehiding motifeme and in this case it was done to protect the treasure until the king could be told of its presence, "and thereupon Sattvaśila went to a corner of the king's courtyard and gave him up the treasure."

But, on the other hand, Rehiding could be done in Jesus' parable for the reasons given in an American true story from a United Press dispatch in *The New York Times* for Sunday, August 16, 1942.

> Discovery of a century-old treasure trove buried at Pilgrim's Beach at Plymouth, Mass., was revealed today by Ben Lay. Mr. Lay said that he and his son, Fred, were skipping stones at the beach a few weeks ago when the son picked up an old silver dollar. They soon found several more coins and then noticed the corner of an old box protruding from the sand. Without attracting the attention of hundreds of bathers in the vicinity, *they covered the spot with sand and went away*. They returned and salvaged all the coins that the box contained.

My italics again emphasize the Rehiding motifeme and in this instance it was to ensure its safety until the finders could obtain it exclusively for themselves. Here, however, it was a case of Finding but Not in Owned Place (as in Horace's parable) and the Rehiding was to stop others from grabbing the treasure from them.

So, then, the subordinate motifeme of Rehiding holds open the intention of the finder and thus the eventual outcome of Jesus' parabolic plot.

3.115 *Selling All One Has*

No parallel motifeme from world treasure tradition which I have found goes quite as far as Selling *All* in the context of hidden treasure. The closest I have found to such *All* is given in the following three motifemic connections.

(1) Seeking and Selling All. When Selling All appears as a submotifeme of Seeking there are, as usual, two obvious sequences: (i) Selling All, Seeking, Not Finding; (ii) Selling All, Seeking, Finding.

The former sequence is found, predictably (§1.53), in a North American story (Driscoll: 3–35) concerning "The Treasure of Oak Island" on the east coast of Nova Scotia and Frederick L. Blair's search for the treasure hidden there by Captain Kidd. I shall simply cite some key passages from the story and let them speak for themselves, but with my italics.

> [1893] Frederick L. Blair was a young insurance salesman. At the age of seventeen he first invested his savings in the projected

company. . . . Young Blair put more and more of his savings into
the treasure company of the day. When he came into money of his
own, *all of the cash and credit he could muster* went to the purchase
of stock from stockholders who were becoming discouraged. . . .
[1895] Frederick L. Blair was one of those who came forward with
more money at this time. He had come into a fortune, and knew of
no better way of augmenting it than by investing in this same thing.
[1897]Blair had assumed much of the responsibility for the
operations, and was more heavily interested financially than any
other stockholder. . . . When accounts were settled up, the control
of the treasure site was vested in Blair.

After all that money and all that digging, Blair must admit: "It is true
that I have put my life and all my earnings into it, and I did not get the
treasure."

And the latter sequence, that of Selling All, Seeking, and Finding,
appears, possibly with equal predictability in a South American story
concerning Lieutenant George Williams, a British subject in Panama
(Driscoll: 136–39):

Williams is a lone worker. . . . [who] has been in the treasure-
hunting business ever since the close of the World War, when he
retired to civilian life, practically broke. But during the war he had
been experimenting with radio. . . . He spent *all the money he
could earn*, carrying on these experiments. He landed at Panama
with his electrical machine for locating metals under the earth, but
he had no money in his pocket. He went out and located and dug up
enough gold to get himself started.

And, we are told, Williams "digs up golden treasures that would turn
the head of King Croesus himself."

(2) Finding and Selling All. In a Japanese treasure tale (Dorson,
1975:245–51) the Selling All is combined with the motifeme of
Finding. The man knows exactly where the treasure is buried. It is "in
the garden behind the mansion of the richest man in Osaka" but he is
so poor ("we don't even have enough money to live on") that Selling
All would hardly help and he borrows the money. from his wife's
relatives to make the trip to Osaka. I shall leave him there for the
moment as this story's conclusion will have to be considered later on
(§3.12).

(3) Obtaining and Selling All. Like the preceding situation, this is

not quite a Selling All but it is as close to it as I could find. In a Chinese folktale (Graham: 253–54) an orphaned beggar

> went into a cave on a big cliff to live. Every night he slept on a big rock. He said, 'Let me roll this stone away.' When he pushed, he noticed that it moved a little, but he could not push it away. Then he went and found an iron bar belonging to a carpenter, and brought it to move the stone. He shoved and pushed the stone away. When the stone had been rolled away, under the earth there was a house that was made entirely of gold and silver. Inside the house everything was to be found.

But in another folktale with similar content (Graham: 283–84) a poor and lazy peasant determines to build himself a house where there is a large stone slab.

> He saw that that stone was very long. So he went and borrowed the stonemason's iron bar and pried on the stone. When he had shoved it aside, he looked below it. Inside was everything. There was a big house, wine, meat, silver, gold, and clothing. . . . There was every kind of thing. He came out and closed the door. He then went and bought the iron lever from the Chinese stonemason. *He wanted to buy it even if it cost a great deal of money.* He bought the lever. (my italics)

Of these four stories, the first two are fairly good parallels to Jesus' motifeme of Selling All but in connection with Seeking, and the last two are as close as I can find for "Selling All" in the context of Finding and Obtaining. That final Chinese story has a combination similar to Jesus's sequence in its conjunction of Rehiding, Paying Much (even if not Selling All), and Obtaining the treasure.

3.116 *Buying the Field*

This concerns Buying the Field *after* Finding the treasure in it, as a (sub)motifeme of Obtaining the trove. In Jesus' tale we are finally certain about the finder's intentions in Rehiding and Selling All. It was directly to buy the field and, thereby, indirectly to obtain the treasure for himself.

During the writing of this book I was very much aware that it might have been done by placing Jesus's story against the background of international *case-law* instead of placing it against the background of international *folk-lore*. And in the present motifeme these two sources make an interesting combination. And here I am referring strictly to the situation where a buyer has *already* found the treasure and has purchased the land *in order* to appropriate it as his own.

(1) Case-Law. Legal traditions where the government claims all of such treasure for itself make any discussion of buyer's or seller's, finder's or owner's rights quite academic. Such is "the regality system, which seems to emerge full-blown in English records of the late eleventh or early twelfth century, a survival of something not specifically German, but common to the Germanic and Scandinavian and perhaps even the Celtic stock; a survival, in fact, of what was probably universal in the primitive stages of society, but was wiped out in those lands which fell under the overwhelming influence of the Roman Law" (Hill: 185). But when one turns to those legal traditions which give the finder some or all right to the treasure, this specific case of deliberate *foreknowledge* presents special problems.

Two examples will suffice. First, stemming from Roman Law, there is this summation:

> If I, knowing that there is a treasure in your land, of which you are ignorant, buy the land from you, and the land, owing to the presence of the treasure, is worth more than double the price that I have paid, it is equitable that you may claim rescission of the contract, or payment of the just price, or that you should receive half the treasure. For if I had found the treasure while the land was still your property, you could have claimed half of it.
>
> Hill: 46

Second, by Prussian law (Hill: 99): "If, however, the buyer knew of the existence of the hidden treasure, and did not inform the seller, he can only count as finder" (i.e., he gets half). It should be noted that it does not at all suffice to argue that "the owner of the field had no rights in the treasure" (Derrett: 13) since he did not even know of its existence. Hill (99, n.4) summarizes on that argument as follows.

> The owner of land has no rights to undiscovered treasure. But the fact that the buyer knows of the treasure before purchase implies that it has already been discovered (and with finding the land-owner's right comes into existence, even, according to one view, if

the treasure has not been lifted); or else it is not treasure in the
proper sense.

(2) Folk-Lore. Even though litigation might eventuate in reversed
decisions, such case-laws agree with the general attitude of the
folktales on the same subject. Unless, of course, the seller is very evil
or very stupid, the buyer with foreknowledge of treasure is not at all
the same as the buyer who subsequently finds treasure on bought
land. The folktales usually manipulate our sympathy towards the
seller and not the buyer in such cases of bad faith.

A first example is found in a Chinese story (Eberhard: 194–95)
about "a miserably poor mason who was fated to remain poor all his
life." His ex-wife remarried to affluence and she gave him "some
sesame cakes, in each of which she hid a piece of money." Since the
mason was not informed of her generosity he gave one cake to an
acquaintance "and the other man found the money inside. He talked
to the mason, and eventually persuaded him to sell them for a small
sum." When he had found out his loss "he took his own life. But the
ruler of heaven took pity on his miserable existence and appointed
him deity of the kitchen in recognition of his goodness and honesty."

The positive apotheosis in that Chinese story receives a negative
counterpoint in the following Indian folktale (Tawney-Penzer: 2.87–
88) and taken together they are a good indication of folklore's general
disapproval of Buying with such malice aforethought. A wife whose
gambling husband had wasted their wealth left him and returned to
her father in a different town. The repentant husband followed her
there intending to request some new capital from his father-in-law.
But on arriving at the town near nightfall he glimpsed a young
merchant and his estranged wife entering a shop and bolting the door.
Listening outside he heard this conversation between his wife and her
lover.

> Listen; as I am so fond of you, I will today tell you a secret: my
> husband long ago had a great-grandfather named Vīravarman; in
> the courtyard of his house he secretly buried in the ground four jars
> of gold, one jar in each of the four corners. And he then informed
> one of his wives of that fact, and his wife at the time of her death told
> her daughter-in-law, she told it to her daughter-in-law, who was my
> mother-in-law, and my mother-in-law told it to me. So this is the
> oral tradition in my husband's family, descending through the

mothers-in-law. But I did not tell it to my husband though he is poor, for he is odious to me as being addicted to gambling, but you are above all dear to me. So go to my husband's town and buy the house from him with money, and after you have obtained that gold come here and live happily with me." [The husband, Devadāsa,] went thence quickly to the city of Pāṭaliputra, and after reaching his house he took that treasure and appropriated it. Then that merchant, who was in secret the paramour of his wife, arrived in that country on pretence of trading, but in reality eager to obtain the treasure. So he bought the house from Devadāsa, who made it over to him for a large sum of money. Then Devadāsa set up another home, and cunningly brought back that wife of his from the house of her father-in-law. When this had been done, that wicked merchant, who was the lover of his wife, not having obtained the treasure, came and said to him: "This house of yours is old and I do not like it; so give me back my money and take back your own house."

They end up in litigation and, when the king hears the whole story, the scheming lover is punished by the loss of all his property. Another version of this story is found in the Kashmiri tale of "The Young Gambling Merchant" (Knowles: 272–96) and here also the would-be treasure purchaser ends up by losing all his wealth and all his goods. These two tales are very good examples of how such schemers are rightly out-schemed in most treasure folktales containing this particular (sub)motifeme of Buying property with foreknowledge of a hidden treasure.

3.12 *Morality in Jesus' Parable*

The actions of the treasure finder in Jesus' parable can now be placed against the general moral background of trove folklore. Stith Thompson (1951:130) has summed up the wider situation as follows. "For the whole area of Europe and the Near East it seems to be a well established characterisitic of the folktale that in such conflicts good shall eventually triumph and wickedness receive a fitting punishment." This principle is very evident when treasure tradition is viewed synchronically. Positively, certain tales and tale-types indicate when one can take another's hidden treasure and, negatively, others indicate when this should not be done by telling how the taker was punished.

First, then, the finder can take another's treasure as long as the story has placed us carefully on the finder's side and against the former owner. Hence the owner must be very evil, very rich, very mean, very greedy, or, indeed, very stupid. And, correspondingly, the finder will usually be very good, very poor, very generous, very nice, or, indeed, very smart. As always, of course, the trickster and the dupe have their own special morality in folklore.

A few examples will suffice. It is quite acceptable to take the treasure of a *scoundrel*, or of those who obtained their treasures by robbing others. The best incidence of this is the story of "Ali Baba and the Forty Thieves" which has been summarized (Aarne-Thompson: #676) as follows:

> Open Sesame. A poor man observes robbers who enter into a mountain . . . uses, like them, . . . the words 'Open Up' and gets gold from the mountain. . . . His rich brother tries to do the same thing but is killed. . . . The rich brother lends his money scales to the poor brother; a piece of money remains in the scales and thus betrays the secret. . . . When he is in the mountain he forgets the formula for opening it.

Hence the motif of "unsuccessful repetition" (§1.54) reappears again in this tale-type but here it is more important to note that while the good or poor brother may rob the robbers, his bad or rich brother may not, usually under pain of death for trying. So in India (Knowles: 267–71) and in Europe (Bolte-Polívka: 3.137) as well as in North (Gardner: 140–45) and South America (Pino-Saavedra: 140–45,266–67), as this story has travelled around the world.

It is also acceptable to take the treasure of a *miser*. An American folktale (Dorson, 1975:493–98) begins thus:

> There was two brothers live in the same village. One was very rich, a bachelor. He wouldn't marry anyone because he was too stingy to support any children. His name was Alexander. The other brother was name Steve. He was so poor he didn't have nothing to eat. And he had twelve children.

Although neither Steve nor Alexander is exactly a model of general virtue in this marvelously scatalogical story, the teller carefully conditions us so that when poor Steve robs rich Alexander's buried treasure there is no question on whose side our judgment must fall.

It is also acceptable to rob the treasure of a *fool* although here again folklore's ambiguous attitude to the fool asserts itself. Well, at least, one may certainly steal a fool's treasure if he is also greedy, stingy, or a miser. So in Indian folktales (Jethabhai: 173–75; Dexter: 77–81).

Second, there are those tales where the taking of another's treasure fails or is punished and the tale places us against the finder. This is also a tale-type:

> *The Poor Brother's Treasure.* The poor brother tells his dream to his rich brother: in a certain place lies a gold treasure. . . . The rich brother tries to pick it up: dung. When he angrily throws his find in to his brother's house, the dung turns to gold.
>
> Aarne-Thompson: #834

Once again you will note that the terms "poor" and "rich" dictate the moral judgment of the story. There is also a Russian folktale (Ralston: 23–26) about a priest who scares a poor widower out of his recently discovered treasure by dressing in a goatskin and pretending to be the Devil. But when he gets home with his stolen hoard he finds that "the goatskin had united with his body all round. And all that they [he and his wife] tried, all that they did, even to taking the money back to the old man, was of no avail."

Or, again, there are two Japanese variants of a taletype already mentioned (§3.115[2]), "*Dream of Treasure Bought*" (Aarne-Thompson: #1654A) which illustrate this folktale treasure morality in their very differences. In one version (Eberhard: 157–60) the seeker is employed in the home of the rich man in whose garden the treasure lies buried according to the dream. *He does not tell the owner his intentions.* But although nothing is said against the owner unless it be that he is rich, much care is taken to stress the industry ("every day he worked faithfully") and patience ("young man never gave up hope and patiently waited") of the seeker. Indeed, he even works for another half-year after finding the treasure. While this is certainly more guile than zeal, the story keeps us on his side and does so very delicately throughout. The second version (Dorson, 1975:245–51) is a story whose beginning was considered earlier as an example of "Selling All" (3.115[2]). It concerns the man whose poverty is such that he must borrow money to make the trip to where the treasure is located. But in this instance *he does tell the man his intentions.* When the owner tries to grab the treasure for himself it disappears and precedes the seeker home to his own house.

Finally, there is the German folktale (Pauli: 1.202–3) about the rich and pious man who gave so much alms to the poor and assistance to pilgrims in the name of God that he came eventually to evil days. In his poverty "a voice" came to him in the night ordering him to swap vineyards with his neighbor and take the treasure buried therein. He does this without notifying the neighbor of his purpose and is soon back helping the poor once again. Both his earlier and latter piety and the divine command implicit in the dream situation are carefully noted before it is acceptable to take another's land in order to secure a hidden treasure. So also, in *The Life of Apollonius of Tyana*, 6.39 (Conybeare: 2.132–35), the sage buys a field containing a treasure from one "who had amassed a fortune in the most unrighteous manner" (but allowing even him one third profit!) and gives it to a man who "was sacrificing to mother Earth in hope of finding a treasure, and he did not hesitate to offer a prayer to Apollonius with that intent." Once again virtue can take vice's hidden treasure.

It is now possible to draw some conclusions on Jesus' parabolic plot against the general moral background of international treasure tradition. First, Stith Thompson's judgment, cited above, means that folklore culture does not approve of taking another's treasure, even treasure hidden on another's land and unknown to the land's owner, *unless* it is established in the story that the loser is not worthy of our approval. "Good" prevails over "bad," however this dichotomy is manifested: poor rich or generous/greedy or even wily/stupid. Second, all six motifemes of Jesus' story have parallels across world folklore but their combination does not fit into the international folklore morality thus noted. We are given no reason to be *against* the field's owner and *for* the treasure's finder and therefore his wily deception of the owner is quite anomalous in treasure tradition. We might have expected, at least, an opening such as this: "which a *poor worker* found" and a conclusion such as this: "and buys that *rich man's* field." Or we could have had a trickster-dupe situation like that in Jesus' parable of The Unjust Steward in Luke 16:1–7 where an owner stupid enough to let a discharged manager draw up the final accounting gets taken as he deserves to be taken in the process. Third, the motifeme of Selling All One Has is probably the most difficult motifeme for which to find exact parallels especially if the emphasis is placed on the All. Fourth, the shock of Jesus' story seems quite deliberate since the *narration* of the plot ensures that only at the very end when we reach the sixth motifeme are we certain that the field belongs to another and that the finder intends to appropriate both field and treasure for himself. The *narration* carefully avoided telling us earlier that the treasure was hidden or found in another's field. So the moral shock of the story is compounded by being delivered abruptly in the final motifeme and the closing phrase. That which was only a possibility in the opening motifeme's "hidden in a field" becomes a surprising certainty in the closing motifeme's "buys that field." And all of this will have to be explained in any adequate analysis of Jesus' treasure parable.

3.2 Jesus' Parable and Jewish Treasure Stories

The next step is to contrast Jesus' story with the wider Jewish treasure tradition of which it is a part but a part whose difference from the rest requires special attention. I shall use the same two rubrics of motifemes and morality as in the preceding section.

3.21 *Jesus' Parable and Jewish Motifemes*

In *Figure 6* above (§2.31) I gave the stemma for the earlier and more specific series of Jewish treasure parables. This will be repeated here as the simplest way to underline how Jesus' treasure plot has deviated from the closest ones in his tradition, as in *Figure 8.*

Figure 8.

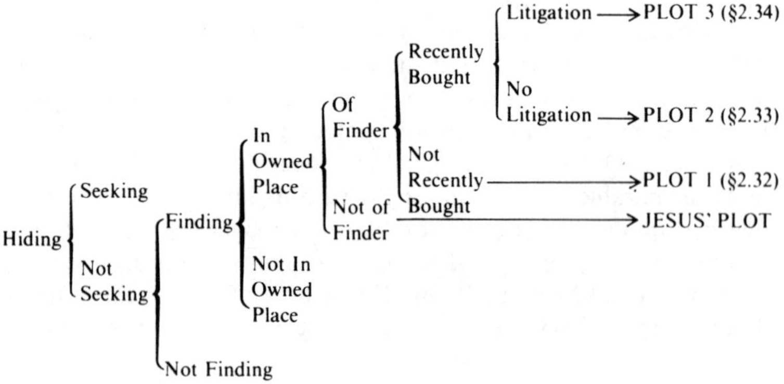

As seen before, Jesus' first motifeme, Hiding in the Earth, starts the story down the most obvious path in all of treasure tradition. His second one, Not Seeking, continues the story along the more standard of the two major possibilities for this stage. He chooses the route of Hiding, Not Seeking, Finding, and in this selection he remains utterly within one's expectations for the Jewish tradition in which he lived. But the third motifeme, Finding in Another's Land, takes a most unexpected turn. You will recall, of course, that this is third in canonical motifemic sequence but that the key sub-unit of In Another's Land is withheld by the story's plot narration until the sixth and last (sub)motifeme. Of the two options, then, In Owned Place, or, Not In Owned Place, Jesus' parable ignores the option chosen, for example, by Horace (§3.113) and elects instead that taken by Philo and the Jewish treasure tradition in general. But then, immediately, comes the first surprise in the selection of options: In Owned Place, *but*, Not of Finder. The Finding, in other words, is not on the finder's own land.

At this point Jesus' story has departed the guiding plot decisions of his own tradition and the story is on its own. This point may be emphasized by a specific comparison between his final motifeme as the story clarifies and climaxes its development and a very similar motifeme in the other Jewish folktale, "Parted and Reunited" (Bin Gorion: 3.1046–49).

The story is somewhat modelled on the Job theme and I would underline how carefully the finder's piety has been established before the Buying takes place and, even then, it is done only at divine command. "Once there was a pious man who never swore a false oath in his life. Indeed, he never swore an oath at all, even regarding the truth. He was very wealthy." He passes on to his son both his piety and his wealth and the son promises the dying father never to take an oath. Soon the tricksters descend on him demanding money that they falsely claim his father had owed them, "Or else let him take oath to the contrary and he would be free of them." Holding to his piety and his promise, "the orphan" ends up "a complete pauper" and is finally imprisoned for debt. His "saintly wife" redeems him thence but she and his children are kidnapped into slavery and the poor orphan ends up as a naked beggar in a strange land. Finally, as the story hits rock-bottom, he is ready to commit suicide, but:

> He turned about and saw the likeness of an angel who said to him:
> "Come here, for a treasure has been waiting for you at this place all

these years. Take this treasure, which I have kept for you, for now
your appointed time has come to succeed because you kept your
father's command and never swore an oath." Then he showed him
the treasure and said to him: "Go and buy this river from the lord of
the land and afterwards build a big city here." And so the man did,
going to the lord of the land and saying: "My lord, are you prepared
to sell me this river from such and such a place to such and such a
place?" "You foolish fellow," said the lord to him, "what will you do
with it?" "Even so," he answered, "sell it to me!" The lord of the land
sold him the river for a great deal of money, and gave it to him at
once and wrote it over to him with witnesses, in everlasting and
absolute sale.

Soon the man is himself a king, his children and (untouched) wife are
returned to him, and the story terminates with citations from Exod
20:6 and especially 20:7, "You shall not take the name of the Lord
your God in vain!"

It would be most unseemly and discourteous, of course, to wonder
where he had obtained that "great deal of money" to buy the river and
its hidden treasure from the unsuspecting king. The parable has other
purposes than total narrative credibility and these purposes are very
carefully orchestrated. Before the man is allowed to take the treasure
by Buying its location with deliberate foreknowledge, the story has
established: (1) his extraordinary piety for which he has suffered
extraordinary privations: all his property, his family, his clothes, and,
almost, his life by suicide; (2) that the treasure was preserved there for
him and always intended for him alone; (3) that the Buying is done by
specific angelic command. And, unless it is ungracious to add, (4) that
"a poor Jew" can despoil a pagan king at least once in a while instead
of the reverse all the time! All of which is in stark contrast with Jesus'
story on precisely this same motifeme of Buying another's property
with foreknowledge of its hidden treasure.

3.22 *Jesus' Parable and Jewish Morality*

Where most of the Jewish treasure parables opted for Finding on
the finder's own land, Jesus' story located its treasure on that of
another. And while Buying led to Finding in Plots 2 and 3 of that
tradition, Jesus had Finding lead to Buying in his parable. Thus the
shock of Jesus' parable is even more acute against a Jewish

background than against that of international treasure tradition in general.

J. D. M. Derrett (1) has argued that the "moral quality of the tale seems to be unnecessarily questionable" and that the "parable perplexes because the finder, in buying the field without revealing the presence of the treasure, has apparently taken a mean, or even dishonest, advantage of the owner of the field." Derrett's own conclusion (13) is that the finder's actions are perfectly legal: "Since the owner of the field had no rights in the treasure there was no reason whatever why he should be told of it." He interprets the situation as that of a day-laborer or servant who (a) cannot lift the treasure while in the land-owner's employment or he would be acquiring it for his employer but who (b) can leave the master's employment and then return and take the treasure for himself.

But two very separate legal and moral problems are here confused. First problem: is the find ownerless and how is that determined? Second problem: *granted it is ownerless,* can an *employed* servant lift such an ownerless find for himself or will all such serendipity during employment accrue to the employer? The places in the *Babylonian Talmud* (Daiches-Freedman), such as *b. B. Meṣ.* 10a or 12b or 118a, which Derrett cites, are interested in that second problem, for example in 118a: "Raba raised an objection against R. Naḥman: That which is found by a labourer [whilst working for another] belongs to himself. When is that? If the employer had instructed him, 'Weed or dig for me to-day.' But if he said to him, 'Work for me to-day' [without specifying the nature of the work], his findings belong to the employer!" One may or may not be satisfied with that legal decision, whose brackets by the way are not from me, but it is clear that it concerns *ownerless objects* and considers rights of employment directly and rights of true ownership only indirectly.

The first problem is, however, far more difficult and we have already seen something of its complications (§3.116[1]). And it is this first problem, rather than the cases cited by Derrett, that is the difficulty with Jesus' parable. *Is the discovered treasure ownerless so that the finder becomes the legal and moral owner?* Derrett is actually caught in a dilemma by the plot of Jesus' story. *If the treasure belongs to the finder, buying the land is unnecessary. But, if the treasure does not belong to the finder, buying the land is unjust.*

The question of what is "ownerless" is handled with extreme and even scrupulous care in the Jewish tradition. One example will indicate the moral care and ethical concern devoted to this question. In the *Babylonian Talmud* (Daiches-Freedman), in *b. B. Meṣ.* 25a, the problem concerns the discovery of *only three coins* and the question is how to decide if they are left or lost, owned or ownerless. The principle is, "If a man finds scattered coins, they belong to him. If they are arranged pyramid-wise he is bound to proclaim them." And if one wants to discuss further and ask: "What if they were disposed in a circle, in a row, triangularly, or ladderwise?" the answer is, "Wherever a chip can be inserted whereby they [the coins] may be lifted simultaneously, a proclamation must be made." Once again, behind the varied and refined distinctions, the principle is quite clear and consistent. If the coins evince deliberate intention in their disposition and could thus be identified legally by a claimant, the finder must proclaim the discovery to the community.

In his fascinating study of international treasure law, Sir George Hill (277) has summed up the Jewish law at a much later date as follows:

> The Jewish law, i.e., the Mosaic-Rabbinic law, is drawn from the Talmud, and may be summarized here from the Shulḥan ʿArukh of Joseph ben Ephraim Caro, which was completed in 1555 and published ten years later.
>
> "398. Buried, immured, or hidden objects, as to which it is not certainly to be perceived that they are an anciently buried treasure, are not to be regarded as masterless, and the discoverer has not those rights which the finder has to lost things which he finds.
>
> 399. If it is perceptible that the buried objects are an anciently buried treasure they belong to the first person who deliberately appropriates them. If the discoverer is the owner of the soil he acquires by the discovery right of ownership; otherwise the owner of the soil has no part in the treasure.
>
> 400. If the land in which the treasure is discovered has from ancient times not been out of the possession of the family of the present possessor the treasure belongs to the landowners.
>
> 401. If workmen find a treasure it belongs to them. But if the employer has hired the workmen to collect loose objects for him, and they while doing the work find a treasure, it belongs to the employer."

The principle, then, is that the ownership of treasure remains to the original owner or his heirs if they can be traced; otherwise it falls to the finder.

It seems to me that despite its late date this summarizes very well the intention and spirit of the case-laws found earlier in Talmudic tradition and the plots in Jewish treasure folktales as well. It explains the piety of buyer and seller in Plots 2 and 3, but it also follows that Jesus' parable does not fit with either cases or folktales. Certainly the field's owner does not know of the treasure's existence or he would not sell the field without first removing the hoard. But here once again the dilemma must be underlined. If the finder (1) clearly perceives that the treasure is very ancient trove and (2) knows the land has *not* always belonged to the family who presently dwell on it, he could legally and morally, publicly and immediately claim it for himself *without ever having to buy the land*. But, on the other hand, if he does buy the land, the story is signalling that his legal and moral rights were not at all clear and beyond dispute. *Why buy the land if the treasure belongs to the finder?*

3.3 The Meaning of Jesus' Parable

I shall begin with a summary of my interpretation and then argue it in detail. The parabolic protagonist abandons, explicitly, his *goods*, and, implicitly, his *morals* to obtain the treasure. The parabolic challenge of the Kingdom then operates outward in three concentric circles. The innermost and most obvious circle has the Kingdom demand all our *goods* and one thinks of a range from almsgiving to martyrdom. I shall say no more on this point since good commentators have always emphasized it (Kingsbury: 115). But then comes the next and not so evident circle of challenge which threatens to consume our *morals* as well and thereby endangers even that former demand itself. Finally, most enigmatically, vertiginously, and therefore least clearly, comes a third and outermost circle of challenge which threatens the very *parable* which contains it. The Kingdom demands our "all," demands the abandonment not only of our *goods* and of our *morals* but, finally, of our *parables* as well. The ultimate, most difficult and most paradoxical demand of the Kingdom is for the abandonment of abandonment itself.

3.31 *Jesus' Story as Paradox*

The value of PARADOX, which lay implicitly at the heart of world treasure tradition (§1.9), had been explicitly noted for the Jewish tradition by Philo (§2.321) and he had considered this treasure paradox a metaphor for God's relations with the world, at least sometimes ("often"). Jesus' challenge is much more radical. The Philonic paradox has been, first, compounded in a most unusual manner by the selling of all the finder's possessions to obtain that which was not his to take. And, then, this internal paradox in the parable becomes a metaphor for the paradox of the parable itself. It is a metaphor for a far more devastating view of transcendence and of the Kingdom, Jesus' chosen expression for the act or experience wherein and whereby God's dominion is manifested and accepted on earth. One must give up not only one's possessions but also the very process and advice of such giving up. Among the possessions to be abandoned is this parable itself.

The finder gives up everything, and does so with joy, to obtain the treasure. And that, says Jesus, is what the Kingdom is like. One gives up everything to obtain the gift of God. But here a dark shadow appears. If one gives up everything—gives up "all"—and if this "all" be taken seriously, then *one must also give up this parable itself.* One must give up even the advice to give up everything. We have walked, we have been led, straight into a paradox like that of the sign which reads, "Do not read this sign." Did the parable intend this paradox? Did it deliberately force us into paradox to say that the Kingdom can only be revealed "like that"?

It is possible, of course, that the parable was just using language carelessly like the unthinking speaker who serenely assures us, "I'm always wrong," or the unreflecting adviser who tells us, "Trust nobody." It is possible that the parable simply meant "a lot" when it said "all that he has." It is possible that it did not really mean that parables themselves, our very linguisticality and narrativity, must strain, crack, and break before the Kingdom of God. I prefer, however, to take the parable's language with absolute seriousness for three interwoven reasons which I shall separate over the next three sections of this chapter.

3.311 *The Tradition before Jesus*

The first argument concerns the way in which the paradoxical language of Jesus continues, intensifies, and indeed climaxes the deep stream of paradox which flowed through his tradition from its source in the *aniconicity* of Israel's God. I shall not repeat what I have written about this elsewhere (1976a:55–60) but, presuming that, shall add only a postscript to those examples. This interpretation condenses into one dramatic moment what may well have been a longer, slower, but inevitable process within the tradition itself. It may be termed *artistic exegesis* since it combines the license usually accorded that adjective with the validity usually expected from that noun.

At the foot of Mount Sinai the Israelites had grown fearful at the prolonged absence of Moses who was alone with God at the hidden summit of the mountain. In Exodus 32 they had constructed a golden calf, or bull, as a symbol or symbolic throne for the power and fertility which could take them from bondage in Egypt and bring them to the prosperity of the Promised Land. In Exod 32:19–20 Moses descends the mountain,

> and as soon as he came near the camp and saw the calf and the dancing, Moses' anger burned hot, and he threw the tables out of his hands and broke them at the foot of the mountain. And he took the calf which they had made, and burnt it with fire, and ground it to powder, and scattered it upon the water, and made the people of Israel drink it.

In the biblical story, then, Moses breaks first the tablets of the Law which he had brought down from God and then he shatters the golden bull which the people had made. One presumes that the breaking of the tablets is straightforward anger, outrage which smashes whatever is closest and even dearest. The question, "Why did Moses smash both the tablets of stone and the bull of gold?" might not strike one as worthy of serious discussion.

In the early nineteen thirties the Jewish genius of Arnold Schoenberg, returning to his people in the face of imminent holocaust, focused an opera around that precise question. His *Moses und Aron* takes some poetic license with Exodus 32. First, it reverses the sequence of the breakage: the bull is destroyed before the tablets of the Law are shattered; and, second, this allows an important dramatic confrontation to take place between Moses and Aaron in Act II of the opera. All my citations, by the way, are taken from the libretto in the Columbia "Masterworks" rendition (M2-33594).

The brief Scene 4 is given over completely to Moses' destruction of the golden calf: "Begone, you image of powerlessness to enclose the boundless in an image finite." And, at Moses' command, according to the stage directions, "the golden calf vanishes." But in Scene 5 Aaron counter-attacks by pointing to the tablets of the Ten Commandments which Moses is stll holding, in Schoenberg's revisionist version, and accuses him with this: "They're images also," to which Moses has the gracious honesty to respond, "Then I smash to pieces both these tablets, and I shall ask him to withdraw the task given me." This is Schoenberg's interpretation of why Moses shattered both the law of stone and the bull of gold. His reversal of the sequence and his invented dialogue function to make it all dramatically explicit but the text of the Bible itself is open to such a reading since it furnishes us with no reason for the double shattering.

I have two comments on all this. First, both these images of Yahweh can be communicated verbally and/or visually. One can verbalize Yahweh as absolute but amoral power or one can visualize this as a golden bull. One can verbalize Yahweh as absolute but moral law or one can visualize this as commandments carved on stone and brought down from the clouds. The argument, therefore, is not about verbal as against visual images. Second, the debate is not that Aaron's visual/verbal image of amoral power is not as adequate to Yahweh as is Moses' visual/verbal image of moral law. This could well be true but Moses is too theologically honest in Schoenberg's vision to accept such a cheap and inconsistent victory. The problem, as Schoenberg's Moses acknowledges, is that there must be no images of Yahweh, neither visual nor verbal, that God is, in my phrase, absolutely aniconic or, more crudely but possibly more clearly, un-image-able. Therefore, Moses has the last word, or lack of word, as the curtain falls at the end of Act II, Scene 5, of the opera:

Inconceivable God!
Inexpressible, many-sided idea,
will you let it be so explained?
Shall Aaron, my mouth, fashion this image?
Then I have fashioned an image, too, false
as an image must be.
Thus am I defeated!
Thus, all was but madness that
I believed before,

and can and must not be given voice.
O word, thou word, that I lack!

The initial paradox that Moses, the seer, could not speak, and Aaron, the speaker, had not seen, leads to this terminal paradox of the silent prophet. But the paradox of the aniconic God can only be adequately proclaimed by the concomitant paradox of the stuttering or silent prophet. So, the stage directions read, "Moses sinks to the ground in despair."

The problem is quite clear at this point. If there can be verbal images of God, there can also be visual images of God. If there can be verbal/visual images of God, one can legitimately debate between contesting images. But if God is absolutely aniconic so that no verbal/visual imagery is ever possible, then the end of Act II is a draw and both Moses and Aaron are reduced to silence.

But for twenty years Schoenberg hoped and planned a third act for his opera, an act which would vindicate Moses over Aaron, which would render clear the victory of his aniconic vision. But he was unable to do so. He wrote the words for a single scene in which Aaron's death gives Moses a rather hollow victory but he never set even that to music. In 1931 he hoped to do so, according to one of his letters: "I would like to do everything necessary in order to have the opera completed before I return to Berlin." And in 1950, the year before his death, he could still write, if now a little more cautiously: "It is not entirely impossible that I should finish the third act within a year."

For myself I find that I must honor alike both the opera's incompletion and its author's twenty-year hope. This is the final paradox, mirroring that of the stuttering or silent Moses, as this, in its turn, mirrored the paradox of the aniconic God. The unfinishable opera takes its place with all the other great negations which reflect the shining honesty of so much of modern art.

From a dramatic and a musical point of view the opera ended quite brilliantly with the close of Act II. There is, however, one theological comment which must be made on the impasse in which Schoenberg had trapped both Moses and Aaron, on the one hand, and himself as creator and composer, on the other.

The first encounter between Moses and Yahweh takes place in Exod 3:2-3: "And he looked, and lo, the bush was burning, yet it was not consumed. And Moses said, 'I will turn aside and see this great sight, why the bush is not burnt.'" I take this to be an inaugural visualization of Yahweh, the God of Israel, a visual symbol of God. But note that it is paradoxical for both eye and mind. That which burns, is consumed and destroyed; that which is not being consumed, is not burning. This "great sight," then, is a burning but non-consumed bush set against the barren emptiness of the desert. It is an image of the un-image-able-ness of God, an icon of the aniconicity of Yahweh. And this visual paradox is strengthened and compounded by a verbal one a few verses later on. In Exod 3:14 Moses has asked for the name of this God who has just been revealed to him and he receives an answer translated as "I am who I am." I do not consider this translation to be giving an answer but rather a refusal to answer, a declaration of unanswerability. It is not a name concentrating in itself either metaphysical causality or historical control but might best be translated as, "My Name is The Unnamable One." It is thus a verbal paradox presenting to the astonished ears of Moses the same negation just presented to his equally astonished eyes. It should also be noted that this is not just a *temporary* paradox pending later explanation and fuller revelation (Childs: 76) since God adds in Exod 3:15 that "this is my name for ever, and thus am I to be remembered throughout all generations."

This, then, is my first argument for taking Jesus' radical paradox with utter seriousness. There is really no theory of signs, symbols, or semiosis that holds as *visually aniconic* what is *verbally iconic* as if, for example, God could be described as a stern judge or loving father but not visualized plastically as such. It was inevitable, therefore, that this aniconic vision of God would move from visual to verbal semiosis, from statue to story, and from plastic to parabolic image. Either both modes can succeed or both modes must genuflect in failure.

3.312 *The Tradition in Jesus*

My second argument concerns the way in which this understanding of The Hidden Treasure parable may be integrated with *certain* specific trends and interpretations in recent historical Jesus research. And here I shall have to summarize as much as possible since I do not want to repeat what is already easily available in print.

This research has been progressing through three necessarily consecutive phases and is presently poised between the second and the third one.

(1) The Historical Phase. Those scholars who have agreed on the nature of the Jesus tradition in the gospels and who have decided, therefore, on the principle of dissimilarity as the securest and most rigorously negative criterion of differentiation between the historical Jesus' language and its various evangelical revisions, have reached a general consensus on what materials are to be included in the corpus of authentic and original Jesus data. Obviously, both the nature of the materials and the appropriate methods of differentiation are highly controversial, but my own work, which has based itself absolutely on this earlier research, presumes the general validity of its conclusions. I take as a presupposition, in other words, the basic accuracy of the claim that all the titles used of Jesus in the gospels, and most especially the titular use of the Son of Man, are not to be considered as historically original with Jesus. This in no way questions their interpretive validity for the early communities and thereafter but it does claim that they were not used by Jesus of himself. I would also consider that this phase of research was already established and summarized by Norman Perrin over ten years ago (1967).

(2) The Literary Phase. Once this corpus was established and isolated, the next step was to compare it with itself rather than with the traditional and evangelical contexts in which it had been dispersed and interpretively reframed. At this point a serious problem arose in that the historical critics who had so brilliantly and persuasively isolated the Jesus material seemed to become rather banal and inept at explaining the radicality of its images and the formal and material strangeness of its language.

This mode of linguistic strangeness cuts across all the forms of Jesus' language and, indeed, includes many of his actions as well. It requires, first of all, some linguistic sensitivity and some literary sophistication to catch its full presence and not immediately to translate it into normal language and conclude it is saying what, if it was, could have been said more easily and more clearly in other words and different images.

I would underline four different areas in which *literary* analysis of the strangeness of Jesus' words and deeds has been pointing towards

a certain tentative consensus and I shall name them in the order in
which they have received greatest investigation.

First, *parables*. Norman Perrin (1976), once again, has
summarized this phase to about the mid-seventies, with emphasis on
the work of Wilder, Funk, Via, and myself. Second, *aphorisms*,
whether legal, prophetic and apocalyptic, or sapiential. Perrin's
summary of the situation includes both parables and aphorisms and
correlates the conclusions on each. Since then the most important
work is that of Tannehill from whose study I borrowed the quote on
"negative consciousness" as epigraph for this chapter (58, n.14).
Bruce Vawter (539, n.20) has also drawn attention to Gerhard
Lohfink's analysis of Matt 5:32 as a "prophetic parody of law." Third,
dialogues. I am especially interested in those dialogues which are
accompanied by some action of Jesus. Examples would be the
discussion on tribute for Caesar in Mark 12:13–17 or on the
adulterous woman in John 8:1–11. The former has been expertly
analyzed by both Funk (75–92) and Tannehill (171–77) but the latter
dialogue still awaits the treatment it deserves. Pending that time, I
would note here only certain questions. What does the unique
"wandering" history of this presumably canonical unit tell us about
its content? Is this contextual dislocation a metaphor for the
strangeness of its content? Is our uncertainty concerning its place a
mirror for our uneasiness concerning its meaning? Or, again, are we
at all bothered by the fact that Jesus' aphorism abolishes *all* legal
justice as well as *all* moral judgment, unless, of course, they be
administered by those too young or too insane ever to have sinned?
And, finally, what is the correlation between aphorism and action,
between the saying, "Let him who is without sin among you be the
first to throw a stone at her," and the double writing on the ground
which frames it? Is it to say that all we have is human judgments
written on sand which stay only as long as time and the wind will
tolerate them and thus to take from us the security of judgments
etched by the finger of God on the permanence of stone? Fourth,
actions, and these are closely connected with the preceding units. I
intend here those well-known and enigmatic activities of Jesus such
as eating with "sinners" and healing on the Sabbath. These require
much more study than they have received and especially do they
require analysis free from any covert or overt, explicit or implicit
presumption that they can be explained by Christian "excellence" as

against Jewish "decadence," by love as against legalism, by sincerity as against hypocrisy, or by any such solutions born of chauvinism and polemics.

I have used the word "strangeness" to describe the mode of language characteristic of Jesus across all the forms of his speech and the types of his communication as emphasized by these different authors whose analyses and interpretations might not agree on any other single word, be it hyperbole or radicality, parody or paradox. Imagine, for example, that you have heard of someone whose "images . . . all show clear tendencies toward the extreme. . . . caricatures in which an inclination is magnified so that we see it in its most blatant and ridiculous form. . . . clearly hyperbole . . . decidedly odd. . . . assault our common sense with extreme words" (Tannehill: 85); whose language produces "an incongruity which can lead to laughter" (151) at certain times but which can be "gallingly flippant" (176) at other times. When Tannehill so describes Jesus' speech, and I would absolutely agree with his description, or when he talks of its effects in terms of "negative consciousness" (58, n.14), the general discussion is being forced to move to its third phase.

(3) The Philosophical Phase. By this I mean the need to acquire much greater philosophical and theological sophistication to handle adequately these very special linguistic or semiotic aspects of Jesus' historical communication. What, in other words, is the message of one who writes only on sand?

Once again I shall simply note certain indications that the discussion is moving into a third and possibly final phase for this stream of interpretation. There are, of course, various philosophical and theological options available at this point and it is a question of which will prove itself most useful in understanding the type of (in my terms) highly paradoxical words and deeds of Jesus. Examples would be the use of Whitehead's process philosophy by Beardslee, of phenomenological and/or structuralist analysis by Via (1967, 1975), and by Ricoeur (29–148) himself on the parables, and of the Nietzsche-Heidegger-Derrida tradition by myself (1977).

There is also one very special point to be noted here. Many of the scholars mentioned above are making philosophical statements about the form/content or style/substance of language itself in discussing Jesus' own communication and this means that their theories turn backward and reflect on their own style, form, and language itself. An ethics of style and a morality of form come to the fore in such a situation. How does one say something about Jesus' communication in language whose form does not deny what its content claims? For better or for worse, the only two books whose *form* has sought to be metaphorical and whose *style* has sought to be parabolic, while discussing the metaphorical parables of Jesus, are those by Funk and myself (1976a).

This, then, would be my second argument supporting the paradoxical interpretation suggested for Jesus' treasure parable. It fits within the historically established corpus of the original Jesus material; it gives the same challenge to literary analysis as does all the authentic Jesus tradition; and it demands a sophisticated philosophical and theological awareness of one's linguistic presuppositions to handle it with any adequacy. And, above all, it forces one to ask anew what is for me that dominant question in contemporary research on the historical Jesus: what is the relationship between the paradox of Jesus' language and the Kingdom of Jesus' God?

3.313 *The Tradition after Jesus*

My second argument was presented by placing Jesus' treasure parable against *summaries* of work already done. This third one will be presented against *sketches* of work yet to be done.

(1) Parable and Tradition. First, there is the use of Jesus' treasure story in the gospels. Only one version of the parable is recorded in the official Christian scriptures and it is there given in tandem association with the parable of The Pearl in Matt 13:45–46: "Again, the kingdom of heaven is like a merchant in search of fine pearls, who, on finding one pearl of great value, went and sold all that he had and bought it." Both parables speak of Selling *All* to obtain the desired and precious object. Thus in both cases the *abandonment in* the parable is a paradoxical metaphor for the *abandonment of* the parable itself. But there are two differences between the stories which mute the force of the treasure parable by the very tandem presence of the pearl story. The motifemic sequence in this latter case is: Hiding (as it were), *Seeking* rather than Not Seeking, and Finding. This does not resound immediately with the value of (the Finding) PARADOX seen earlier for the treasure tradition (§1.54; §1.9). But there is an even more

important difference. There is no shock of illegality or immorality in the case of the pearl bought openly and legitimately and, therefore, in this case the *shock in* the parable cannot become a metaphor for the *shock of* the parable. Thus, while I have no doubt that both stories stem from the historical Jesus, I suspect that only their present juxtaposition and especially the muting of the treasure story by the pearl parable explains Matthew's willingness to retain the former tale at all.

Second, there are the citations of the treasure parable in the first two centuries of the Christian era (Allenbach). In the early patristic writings there are four allusions to the treasure parable, in Aristides, Tatian, Irenaeus, and Clement of Alexandria. None of these authors cites the full narrative and what seems to have caught their imagination and held their memory is the phenomenon of hidden treasure and its finding and not the method of obtaining the hoard. They ignore, that is, *where* it was discovered and *how* it was actually secured. I do not wish to draw any particular conclusions from this and I do not intend to suggest that they are avoiding the details of the story with some conscious design. It has already been observed (Johnston, 1977) that these writers were much more interested in biblical *types* than in narrative *parables* and often used the latter word for the former phenomenon, so that it is quite characteristic for them to condense *narrative* into *image* or, in the terms I have been using in this book, to emphasize the *theme* but not the *plot*. All of this is but the inevitable reflection of the wider Christian process wherein and whereby the parabler became the Parable (Crossan, 1975:123–28).

The *Apology*, 16, of Aristides (Roberts-Donaldson: 9.278) is the only citation which refers to anything in Jesus's parable beyond the basic motifemes of Hiding and Finding. In praising Christians he says that "they do not proclaim in the ears of the multitudes the kind deeds they do, but are careful that no one should notice them; and they conceal their giving just as he who finds a treasure and conceals it." This presumably refers to the Rehiding (sub)motifeme of Jesus' story. In Tatian's *Address to the Greeks*, 30 (Roberts-Donaldson: 2.77), he says that, "He has become master of all we have by means of a certain 'hidden treasure,' which while we are digging for we are indeed covered with dust, but we secure it as our fixed possession. He who receives the whole of this treasure has obtained command of the

most precious wealth." Irenaeus, in his *Against Heresies*, 2.26
(Roberts-Donaldson: 2.496), says that "Christ is the treasure which
was hid in the field, that is in this world (for 'the field is the world'
[Matt 13:38]); but the treasure hid in the Scriptures is Christ, since he
was pointed out by means of types and parables." Clement of
Alexandria's *Who Is the Rich Man that Shall be Saved,* 17 (Roberts-
Donaldson: 2.595–96) distinguishes between a good treasure and an
evil one, following Matt 12:34–35, and concludes: "As then treasure is
not one with Him, as also it is with us, that which gives the
unexpected great gain in the finding, but also a second, which is
profitless and undesirable, an evil acquisition, hurtful."

One might generalize to say that Christ, Christianity, Christian life,
or Christian faith is the "hidden treasure" which must be grasped but
that the precise details of the narrative in the original parable are
quite ignored. And, apart from Aristides' mention of Rehiding, the
only motifemes noted are the minimum ones of Hiding and Finding.
If Jesus' parable had been lost, one could hardly reconstruct it from
these brief allusions. Indeed, if we did not know of its existence, it
would be difficult to prove these citations were referring to a
particular parabolic plot and not just to a general narrative theme.

The situation is more interesting in the case of the pseudepigraphal
acts or gospels under varying degrees of gnostic influence. Allenbach
cites three places where there is a conjunction between the images of
the pearl and the treasure, and all three are in that sequence, the
opposite to the Matthean order.

In the *Acts of Peter*, 20 (Hennecke-Schneemelcher: 2.303), it is said
that in "this Jesus you have, brethren, the door, the light, the way, the
bread, the water, the life, the resurrection, the refreshment, the pearl,
the treasure . . ." and in the *Acts of John*, 109 (2.256) Jesus is hymned
as follows: "We glorify thine entering of the Door; we glorify thy
Resurrection that is shown us through thee; we glorify thy Way; we
glorify thy Seed, thy Word, thy Grace, thy Faith, thy Salt, thine
inexpressible Pearl, thy Treasure . . ." In both these very similar
series, *narratives* have been condensed into *images* and *parables* have
become contracted into *titles*.

But by far the most interesting case is the gnostic *Gospel of
Thomas*, 76 and 109, from Nag Hammadi (Guillaumont). All the
preceding citations of the treasure parable were scarcely more than
passing allusions. In no case had anyone given the full text. But four

major points must be noted concerning the use of the parable in this gospel. First, the two parables are there separated from one another as logia 76 and 109. Second, logion 76 is the parable of The Pearl and it is a close parallel to that in Matt 13:45-46. Third, logion 109 is the parable of The Hidden Treasure *but* it is here parallel to the Jewish second plot (§2.33) and not at all parallel to the parabolic plot of Jesus. Fourth, in the context and within the same logion as the story of The Pearl there is a treasure aphorism (=Matt 6:19-20; Luke 12:33). The situation can be indicated in parallel columns as following:

Gos. Thom. 76	Matt 13:44-46
	Treasure Parable (13:44)
Jesus said: The Kingdom of the Father is like a man, a merchant, who possessed merchandise	Again, the kingdom of heaven is like a merchant
	in search of fine pearls, who, on
and found a pearl. That merchant was prudent. He sold the merchandise he bought the one pearl for himself (76a)	finding one pearl of great value, went and sold all that he had and bought it (13:45-46)
Treasure Aphorism (76b)	

This raises the suspicion, and it can hardly be more at the moment, that the tradition had already associated the parables of The Pearl and The Hidden Treasure even before Matthew accepted it (as treasure and pearl) and Thomas rejected it (as pearl and treasure). And also that Thomas (1) replaced the treasure parable with the treasure aphorism because (2) he intended a very different version of that treasure story which was no longer in parallel with that of The Pearl. Notice, by the way, that, on the one hand, Thomas' merchant was *Not* Seeking fine pearls, but that, on the other, Thomas' merchant has no Selling *All*, both as against Matthew's trader.

Be that as it may, what is certain is that Thomas' treasure parable is a variation of the story noted earlier in the Jewish treasure tradition (§2.33) and not a variation of Jesus' parabolic plot (see also Crossan, 1976b):

The Dunghill (*Cant. Rab.*)	The Hidden Treasure (*Gos. Thom.*)
R. Simeon b. Yoḥai taught. [The Egyptians were] like a man who inherited a piece of ground used as a dunghill. Being an indolent man he went and sold it for a trifling sum.	Jesus said: The Kingdom is like a man who had a treasure [hidden] in his field, without knowing it. And [after] he died, he left it to his [son. The] son did not know (about it), he accepted that field, he sold it.
The purchaser began working and digging it up, and he found a treasure there, out of which he built himself a fine palace, etc., etc.	And he who bought it, he went, while he was plowing [he found] the treasure. He began to lend money to whomsoever he wished.

The similarities between the two parables are quite clear as is the purpose of the dissimilarities in Thomas' version. The gnostic story is not interested in indolence as against industry but in ignorance as against knowledge. Hence it has expanded the passing mention of inheritance to a reiterated statement that both the father and son *did not know* about the treasure. Also, there is no mention of the seller's rage at the end of the gnostic version and there probably could not be any such reaction. To rage is to *know* what one has lost.

In summary, then, *it is certain* that Thomas does not have a version of Jesus' parable but rather a gnostic variation on the Jewish second plot. And *it is possible* that Jesus's parable was known to that tradition and deliberately replaced by the alternative Jewish narrative. This means that only one of those seven early citations gives Jesus' parable in full but even it preferred a replacement with a different parabolic plot. Yet this same source found little difficulty in citing Jesus' parable of The Pearl. My suggestion is that the immorality of the finder's actions is the reason for this phenomenon. It is one thing to refer in general to the theme of hidden treasure but it is quite another to record in full the details of Jesus' parabolic plot.

(2) Paradox and Tradition. I have two separate points to make here. First, is the way in which paradox and specifically the paradox of the aniconic God, intensified by Jesus with regard to all modes of communication and all genres of speech, flowed into the Christian tradition which accepted Jesus as its Lord. Bultmann's famous dictum that the Proclaimer became the Proclaimed should be

specified more completely by stating that Jesus, who proclaimed God in paradoxes, became himself proclaimed as the Paradox of God. Indeed, once the shocking paradox of the Cross had become the heart of Christianity, the paradoxes of Jesus' own language started to be muted back to normalcy as examples for moral life or as allegories of historical destiny (Crossan, 1975:89–128).

This perdurance of God's paradoxical aniconicity from the Jewish tradition, through Jesus, into the Christian tradition, touches also on another equally famous aphorism of German scholarship, Ernst Käsemann's dictum that apocalyptic is the mother of Christian theology. Without mentioning Käsemann, John Gager (37) has asked: "What went wrong with early Christianity so that it not only survived the failure of its initial prophecies but did so in spectacular fashion?" My answer to Gager's question is that paradox was even more fundamental than apocalyptic in the tradition and that the latter's failure merely emphasized and enhanced the former's presence and dominance. Following Käsemann's image, as long as the father is paradox, the failures of the mother can hardly stunt the growth of the child.

Second, this deep matrix of paradox inherent in *aniconic* monotheism, which has just been discussed as moving through the Jewish Jesus into the Christian tradition, continued, of course, equally if differently, within the Jewish tradition itself. And this brings up most forcibly the problem so hauntingly and brilliantly posed by Gershom Scholem and so recently reiterated by W. D. Davies. Scholem's beautiful book, massive in size, awesome in scholarship, deeply sensitive to the tragedy it recounts, and profoundly human in rendering it of universal interest and validity, has explicitly raised the necessity of comparing Jesus of Nazareth (792–802) with Sabbatai Sevi (687–93) under the common rubric of paradoxical messiah.

W. D. Davies (530–31) has summarized the events as follows:

Sabbatai Svi was born in Smyrna in 1626. In 1648 he proclaimed himself to be the Messiah, but was met with scorn. Three years later the Jewish community outlawed him. But in 1665 Nathan of Gaza, a young rabbi trained in the talmudic schools in Jerusalem, became convinced, through a vision, that Sabbatai Svi was the Messiah. He persuaded a reluctant Sabbatai of his messianic destiny and proceeded to disseminate the astounding news of his identity throughout the diaspora. The movement spread to Jewish communities in Yemen and Persia in the East and to those in the West as far as England, Holland, Russia, and Poland. It was stirred by massive repentance, expressed in fasts and mortifications, and by extraordinary enthusiasm, visions, and miracles. The date of the end of all things was fixed for 1666 but was conveniently moved when necessary. The antinomian acts of Sabbatai Svi failed to dampen the enthusiasm of the believers, who through him were experiencing the emotional reality of redemption. Neither the astounding apostasy of Sabbatai Svi to Islam and his attempts to persuade believers to apostatize, nor even his death destroyed the movement. There still exist a few believers in Sabbatai Svi.

I shall break Scholem's commentary on all this into three points: (1) the paradox of the apostate messiah; (2) comparison between the paradoxes of the crucified and apostate messiahs; (3) the essentially destructive nature of that latter paradox as compared with the constructive possibilities of the former one.

(a) Sabbatai Ṣevi as Apostate Messiah. Scholem comments (690–92) on this as follows:

> To believe in an apostate messiah was to build one's hope on foundations of paradox and absurdity, which could only lead to more paradoxes. The unity and consistency of rabbinic Judaism were not affected by the one inevitable paradox inherent in it, indeed, in all religion and in human experience itself—that of theodicy and the sufferings of the righteous. The universal character of this anguishing paradox in no wise diminished its seriousness, but it rendered it less destructive. . . . The Sabbatian paradox, however, was not that of a saint who suffers and whose suffering is a mystery hidden with God, but of a saint who sins. . . . For all the farcical absurdity of the sorry denouement, there was something genuinely tragic about it. A national revival, nourished by the tradition and historical experience of many generations, had, for the first time since the destruction of the Second Temple, aroused the entire Jewish people.

(b) Sabbatai and Jesus as Paradoxical Messiahs. Scholem (795) notes that,

> when discussing the Sabbatian paradox by means of which cruel disappointment was turned into a positive affirmation of faith, the analogy with early Christianity almost obtrudes itself. . . . Both

Christianity and the Sabbatian movement took as their point of departure the ancient Jewish paradox of the Suffering Servant which, however, they stressed with such radicalism that they practically stood it upon its head. Both movements gave rise to a mystical faith centered on a definite historical event, and drawing its strength from the paradoxical character of this event.

(c) Constructive and Destructive Paradox. After considering the very instructive parallels between the two paradoxes and between Christianity and Sabbatianism, Scholem (798-99) remarks that,

the structural similarities must not blind us to the profound differences between early Christianity and Sabbatianism. . . . [in] historical background and social realities. . . . An even more important factor is the decisive role played by their respective central personalities. . . . No doubt an apostate messiah constitutes an even greater paradox than a crucified messiah, but the paradox has no constructive value. The doctrine that by betraying his religion the redeemer fulfilled his messianic mission is essentially nihilistic. . . . Unlike the passion and death of Jesus, Sabbatai's apostasy, though surrounded with a tragic halo by Sabbatian literature, was essentially destructive of all value.

All this may very well be true but I am not convinced that Scholem has adequately explained why one paradox leads (or at least led) to nihilism while the other did not. I am not convinced that messianic personality is a sufficient explanation, and I would not want to guess what might have happened had the Turkish authorities been foolish enough to have crucified Sabbatai Sevi instead of having bribed him into apostasy as "Mehemed *kapici bashi oturak*" (Scholem: 686). It seems to me that there is a more profound difference than that of character between the two paradoxical messiahs. Paradox, I would suggest, can only operate humanly and creatively in *negative dialectic* with and against a tradition which is both continually generated by it and also continually regenerated through being undermined by it. The paradox of the apostate messiah did not and possibly could not develop such a tradition and so the paradox was left to feed on itself and thereby turn destructive and nihilistic. The paradox of the crucified messiah, on the other hand, created such a tradition and even claimed it was *a* and even *the* legitimate continuation of the Jewish tradition. In due time, of course, the central paradox came

home to haunt such claims but that took a long time, far too long a
time in which there was much Jewish suffering and very little
Christian self-criticism.

It is now possible to sum up these three arguments for my reading
of Jesus' treasure parable. The deep core of paradox which stemmed
in Judaism from the aniconicity of God was intensified in Jesus'
vision with regard to all the modes of communication and all the
genres of language, and, then, his own paradoxical actions and
aphorisms, dialogues and parables, were themselves consummated
and condensed *for and by* his followers in the supreme paradox of the
Cross. This common core of paradox is thus at the heart of both the
Jewish and Christian traditions and because of this the comparison of
Jesus as crucified messiah with Sabbatai Sevi as apostate messiah is a
profound warning of how such paradoxes may move along the finally
destructive path from apocalypticism through gnosticism and into
nihilism. It is, however, unfortunate that all such warnings,
judgments, and distinctions are usually quite clear by the time it is
also quite late for those who have wagered their humanity on their
veracity and validity.

3.32 *Jesus' Parable as Fundamental Morality*

The problem of the finder's morality in Jesus' parable has already
been raised in terms both of world treasure tales and Jewish treasure
parables. I would like to look at it one final time in the light of the
preceding discussion of Jesus and his tradition, and especially in
terms of nihilism as the permanent danger that paradox might lure
the human imagination to an inhuman end.

3.321 *Jesus' Parables and Practical Morality*

When Jesus' parables are compared, synchronically and
synoptically, with other Jewish parables two striking differences are
immediately evident. First, with regard to *form.* I alluded earlier to
the formal analysis of rabbinical parables by R. M. Johnston (1976).
And we saw examples of this rabbinical format in considering the
three plots of the earlier Jewish treasure parables themselves. In this
form the basic sequence was: illustrand, illustration (parable proper),
and application of illustration to illustrand. And this process was

usually framed and protected by biblical citations before and after it. One of the most disturbing things about the form of Jesus' stories is that there is usually no such clear application or else, where one is present, tradition criticism judges that it does not derive from the historical Jesus. For example, The Bridesmaids (Matt 25:1–13) or The Talents (Matt 25:14–30) clearly enjoins the proper use of money and the prudent care of oil, but what is lacking, from Jesus, is an equally clear application of what the money and the oil illustrates. Second, with regard to *content* and again in contrast with other Jewish parables. I do not deny for a moment that certain parables, The Good Samaritan for example, include morally superior actions of which the story certainly approves, but there are other parables in which the narrated action ranges from self-serving, with The Wedding Guest in Luke 14:7–11, to the immoral, with The Unjust Steward in Luke 16:1–7, to the murderous, with The Wicked Husbandmen in Mark 12:1–12 (for analysis, see Crossan, 1973:69–70, 86–96, 108–111). And, apart even from those ones, the majority have actions which might best be described as morally neutral. In all of this I am presuming the isolation of the original content of these stories as distinct from later traditional or evangelical contexts.

One might easily respond that the *primary* point of these stories is often resolute action or critical decision and that such responses can be illustrated equally well through amoral or immoral or moral actions. This is absolutely correct but it is equally correct that the other Jewish parables tend to prefer *both primary and secondary points(s)* to carry clear moral messages. Two examples: Earlier I compared in parallel columns the Jewish treasure parables of The Dunghill and The Distant Residence whose *primary* point was certainly the contrast between the rage of the Egyptians at having lost the hidden treasure which was the Israelites themselves at the Exodus (§2.33). The Dunghill parable wishes to extend the moral message to a *secondary point* and it explicitly contrasts the indolence of the seller with the industry of the buyer in the story even though these additions do not really fit with the basic allegorical application of the story. Second, this scrupulous moral sensitivity is a feature of the entire tradition even in its final stages of translation and editorial presentation. Compare the openings of two versions of the first Jewish plot concerning Abba Judan, seen before in *Deut. Rab.*, 4.8 (§2.321):

The Dunghill (*Lev. Rab.*, 4.4)	The Dunghill (Deut. *Rab.*, 4.8)
Once R. Eliezer and R. Joshua and R. Akiba went to the Harbour-area of Antiochia, to make a collection for [the support of] scholars. There was a man there of the name of Abba Judan, who used to provide maintenance liberally [for the needy].	Once R. Eliezer and R. Joshua went out on a mission to gather funds for a charitable cause. They came to the valley of Antiochia, where was a man, Abba Judan by name, who was in the habit of giving liberally to our Rabbis.

I am interpreting the phrases within brackets in the left-hand version as necessitated by editorial delicacy lest the collection for scholars be deemed for other than their "support" and lest the liberality of Abba Judan be understood as going to other than "the needy."

When Jesus' parables are viewed, synchronically, against this background of other Jewish parables, they are extremely surprising in both form and content and no distinction of primary and secondary points can dissipate this surprise. Compared to the delicate moral sensitivity and intense ethical concerns of other Jewish parables, Jesus' stories evince a very different emphasis. I would insist that this is a most serious question and that it cannot be avoided by simply discussing only or emphasizing especially those stories, such as The Good Samaritan, whose (for me) secondary point evinces superlative morality. If one took, for instance, the corpus of Jesus' parables and tried to assemble from them a schema of practical morality, one would fail dismally, but exactly the opposite would be true if one took the corpus of other Jewish parables as a reservoir for practical moral guidance.

3.322 *Treasure Parable and Practical Morality*

This general problem is compounded by Jesus' treasure parable in particular. For the purpose of the parable the (sub) motifeme of Selling All was the dominant element. But a storyteller who wished to stress that element could easily have done so *without* involving the (sub)motifeme of Finding on Another's Land. In discussing that former motifeme I already indicated two treasure stories which came close enough to that Selling All motifeme without having the moral problem raised by Buying the Field in order secretly to obtain another's treasure (§3.115). On their analogy, Jesus' parable could have said: (1) "like a man who knew of a treasure in a far country and, going with joy, sold all he had, and travelled there to find the treasure"; or (2) "like a man who knew of a treasure deep beneath the earth and, going with joy, sold all he had to buy instruments for digging down to the treasure." It would have been quite simple to have the treasure *Not in Owned Place*, for instance, and still have it necessary to keep the Selling All motifeme.

In the light of Jesus' other parables, aphorisms, and actions in general, and this motifemic sequence of the treasure parable in particular, the question can now be posed *whether the parable deliberately intended to include morality among that "all" which the finder abandoned and therefore also among the "all" which the Kingdom might demand from the hearer.* One recognizes immediately the dangers of such a proposal since it can so easily appeal to adolescent rebellion, to gnostic antinomianism, or even to criminal nihilism. But the question must still be asked and be asked within the general paradox of the parable itself which both tells us that the Kingdom will cost us our morality and then tells us that it will cost us that advice as well. But how else might a teacher suggest that God could overturn our morality without our immediately concluding that immorality is now the highroad to heaven?

3.323 *Fundamental Morality and Practical Morality*

I would maintain, therefore, that Jesus' teaching was not primarily concerned with *practical morality* but with what I would term *fundamental morality.* This is not to dismiss as irrelevant the very real importance, now as then, of such practical problems in morality, but to attempt to ground them in something which transcends them, namely, for Jesus, the Kingdom of God.

I am distinguishing between fundamental and practical (including, of course, speculative) morality on the analogy of the distinction proposed by Martin Heidegger when Jean Beaufret asked him concerning the relationship of ontology and ethics (295–301). "If now, in accord with the basic meaning of the word ἦθος, ethics dwells in the abode of man, then that thought which thinks the truth of Being as the original element of man as existing is already in itself at the source of ethics" (297). Again: "More essential than any establishment of rule is the abode in the truth of Being" (300).

Fundamental morality or ethics, then, concerns our *dwelling* with God and practical morality or ethics concerns our *dwelling* with one another (Crossan, 1973:80–83). To establish the clear primacy and dominion of the former Jesus' language comes dangerously and deliberately close to ignoring the latter completely.

One example may be helpful at this point. In an earlier work (Crossan, 1975:108–19) I had argued more or less the above position concerning Jesus' parable of The Great Feast. There are three extant versions of that story, in Matt 22:1–14; Luke 14:16–24; and *Gos. Thom.* 64, and their very diversity both forces one and assists one in establishing the original version from the historical Jesus, not the exact words, of course, but at least the basic narrative structure. My argument there was that *the original version* was a paradoxical narrative in which invited "friends" (or known and expected people) are absent from a dinner while only "strangers" (or unknown and unexpected people) are present. I stressed that Jesus had made the story quite plausible, in that the host's *sudden* decision on a dinner-party found all his friends or acquaintances reasonably and legitimately busy elsewhere, but by the time the servant returned with the bad news, the host had the dinner ready and simply brought in whomsoever he could find to eat the meal.

Dan O. Via, Jr. (1976:393–94) has commented on the above argument as follows:

> The parable no doubt implies that the original, intended guests, who are finally excluded, are friends and that those finally included are strangers. But the dominant impression arising from the concreteness of the parable is that these invited guests, who are nowhere called friends, have actively neglected a duly extended invitation and those included are the objects of the host's intention to fill his banquet hall. "Friend" is an abstraction from the parable's particular representation of the original guests and discloses the reduction of the latter to a carrier for the structure. And it is, after all, not such a shock to expectations to exclude "friends" like those in the parable. If the manifested unity of surface structure and content is not ignored, I find it hard not to conclude that the parable does make some suggestions about God's intentional action, the kind of response this calls for, and the difficulty of making that response.
>
> I am tempted to say provisionally that parable, at the level of deep structure—the communication axis of the actantial model—

does subvert world but that, at the level of surface-structure-and-content, it hints indirectly at the horizon of a new world and thus approaches myth and/or apologue. This kind of polyvalent versatility is what should be expected of a symbolic story set in the stream of a given religious culture.

In terms of the present discussion Via is insisting that there is practical morality ("horizon of a new world") contained in the parable at least on the level of surface content.

I do not wish to make much of my term "friends." I used it to mean people the host knows, acquaintances, people who would be invited in the normal course of events. However, it must be noted that the *original* invitation, which finds its closest expression in Thomas, *was without warning*, and that the excuses of the first guests, in both Thomas and Luke as against Matthew, are both reasonable and also extremely polite. In the present texts Luke and Matthew make it very clear that the first guests had been previously warned and that their present excuses are therefore unacceptable and this creates a contradiction with the politeness of their refusals in Luke. But in Thomas, which in general is closest to Jesus' original plot, the story is much more internally consistent in that the guests had not been previously warned and thus their very detailed and very polite ("I pray to be excused") refusals are consistent and plausible. All of this points to the utter necessity of first doing careful tradition criticism and thus determining the original narrative content before and if one wishes, as I do, to consider the parable as it was for the historical Jesus.

But Via's point is completely correct for each of the three extant versions. All of them contain quite specific and practical moral instruction both on a personal and historical (allegorical) level. Thomas enlarges the three guests to an unwonted foursome by inserting in first place one who is involved with "merchants" and he adds a moral interpretation at the end: "Tradesmen and merchants shall not enter the places of my Father." This negative moral warning becomes a positive one in Luke 14:21 where the guests are "the poor and maimed and blind and lame." And the incipient allegorizing of Luke's account is consummated in Matthew's version where the guests kill the host's messengers and are severely punished in return (Matt 22:6–7). These three accounts are, in varying ways and degrees, laden with practical morality and I am in complete agreement with

Via on this point. I would even suggest that they contain much more than the "horizon" of a world and that this world is not at all a "new one."

The debate is not really on deep structure as against surface content but on both of these in Jesus' original story as against both of these in the three extant versions. Once again, for example, I would emphasize very much the surface content of the guests' excuses which are given in direct speech, in specific detail, and in most polite terms (Luke and Thomas) so that we can see and even hear that their excuses to the *unexpected* invitation (Thomas) were reasonable and extremely courteous. But I would still argue that it was (1) the total absence of any practical morality in Jesus' original version which (2) allowed and even induced each of the authors to insert and append (3) three quite different practical moral (personal and historical) applications.

One final point. In Luke 14:12–14 Jesus had said, "When you give a dinner or a banquet, do not invite your friends or your brothers or your kinsmen or rich neighbors, lest they also invite you in return, and you be repaid. But when you give a feast, invite *the poor, the maimed, the lame, the blind,* and you will be blessed, because they cannot repay you." That, I would claim, is fundamental but not practical morality. Practical morality says: help, assist, share with, show compassion for the poor, maimed, lame, and blind. This says, and really it is not that difficult at least to *say* it: give alms. But that is not what Jesus said. What he said was absolutely paradoxical and what would most likely happen were it taken literally has been well shown in Luis Buñuel's film *Viridiana.* When Luke tries to make some practical moral sense out of it by interpreting the aphorism through the parable which follows it in his text, he has the emergency guests made up of "the poor and maimed and blind and lame," and thus does the best he can with it. But his interpretation is a far cry from Jesus' radical challenge. Jesus said *not* to invite your friends but to invite the outcasts. Luke says, in his version of the parable, if the dinner is prepared and your friends won't or can't come, invite in the outcasts. Jesus' story did everything it could to exclude practical morality from its plot in order to focus more vividly on the paradoxical message of its fundamental morality. It seems to me to have succeeded brilliantly unless, of course, one wishes to find practical morality in the host's refusal to waste food.

At this point I am very much aware of needing not only more time and more space but also more thought and more help in probing the connection between fundamental and practical ethics or morality. Since I have found it necessary to raise the problem in order to do justice to the challenge of Jesus' treasure story, I would like to conclude with two suggestions on how one's dwelling in the presence of the aniconicity of God might influence the deeply serious question of practical morality.

First, the essential force of divine aniconicity is *negative* rather than positive. It robs us of our absolutes and in the space cleared by their absence offers us a freedom for human responsibility, personal and social decision, and the creation of those conventions which make us what we are. Aniconicity does to us what the blank page does to the writer, everything and nothing, but the former only because of the latter. Second, this negation, withdrawal, and absence, effected in the depths of our imagination, generates a probing restlessness which is as dangerous as it is dynamic and which disturbs old answers not so much because they are old as because they are answers. This creativity, for morality as for everything else, is the most precious gift of divine aniconicity.

There are, then, three points here that require much more thought than I can presently give them. What is the relationship between fundamental morality, dwelling with God, and speculative-practical morality, dwelling with one another, *in the light of divine aniconicity*? What is the relationship between the paradoxical communications of Jesus concerning the Kingdom of God and that first problem? What is the relationship of Jesus' treasure parable to the two preceding problems?

3.33 *Jesus' Story as Metaparable*

The purpose of this final section is to suggest a specific name for the type of paradoxical parable I have found in Jesus' treasure story. I had tended in earlier discussions of Jesus' parables to analyze them along similar lines of enigma and paradox but, in calling them "parables," I had sought to restrict that term to them alone while using some other term, such as "examples" or "allegories," for those other Jewish parables which have both a striking similarity and an even more striking dissimilarity with them. I am now seeking some more exact terminology for expressing this combination of similarity and dissimilarity not only for Jesus' parables but for many of the other forms of speech and modes of action associated with him.

3.331 *Rhetoric and Dialectic*

In a recent study, which is as clear as it is persuasive, Stanley E. Fish has proposed a very basic distinction between what he terms "rhetoric" and "dialectic." At the start of his book (1–2) he distinguishes between them as "two kinds of literary presentation" and describes what he means as follows:

> A presentation is rhetorical if it satisfies the needs of its readers. The word "satisfies" is meant literally here; for it is characteristic of a rhetorical form to mirror and present for approval the opinions its readers already hold. It follows then that the experience of such a form will be flattering, for it tells the reader that what he has always thought about the world is true and that the *ways* of his thinking are sufficient. This is not to say that in the course of a rhetorical experience one is never told anything unpleasant, but that whatever one is told can be placed and contained within the categories and assumptions of received systems of knowledge.
>
> A dialectical presentation, on the other hand, is disturbing, for it requires of its readers a searching and rigorous scrutiny of everything they believe in and live by. It is didactic in a special sense; it does not preach the truth, but asks that its readers discover the truth for themselves, and this discovery is often made at the expense not only of a reader's opinions and values, but of his self-esteem. If the experience of a rhetorical form is flattering, the experience of a dialectical form is humiliating.

Towards the end of the book (378) he again distinguishes them but on a much deeper level. They represent, he says,

> an opposition of epistemologies, one that finds its expression in two kinds of reading experiences: on one side the experience of a prose that leads the auditor or reader step-by-step, in a logical and orderly manner, to a point of certainty and clarity; and on the other, the experience of a prose that undermines certainty and moves away from clarity, complicating what had at first seemed perfectly simple, raising more problems than it solves. Within this large opposition there are, of course, distinctions to be made. . . . but in general the contrast holds, between a language that builds its readers' confidence by building an argument they can follow, and a

language that, by calling attention to the insufficiency of its own procedures, calls into question the sufficiency of the minds it unsettles.

Thus, his distinction of rhetoric and dialectic involves a distinction of "epistemologies," thence a distinction of "literary presentation," and, thence, finally, a distinction of "reading experiences." His corpus of investigation is primarily seventeenth century English literature although he traces the distinction back to Plato, Augustine, and the Neoplatonists. The distinction cuts across several genres within his chosen corpus and here, for one example, is how he applies it to Puritan, as rhetorical, and Anglican, as dialectical, sermon traditions (75):

> in one the faculties are put in good working order and made answerable to the task of comprehending truth; in the other the faculties are first broken and then replaced by the object of their comprehension, "a kind of saving by undoing"[Milton]; one makes linguistic forms serviceable by making them unobtrusive; the other thrusts the forms of language before us so that we may better know their insufficiency, and our own; one claims only to convey the truth and therefore claims everything; the other begins by claiming everything and then presides over the gradual disallowing of all its claims; one invites us to carry the truth away, the other to be carried away by the truth.

Finally, he sums up the entire process by concluding that (371),

> In all of these works, an uncomfortable and unsettling experience is offered as the way to self-knowledge, in the hope that self-knowledge will be preliminary to the emergence of a better self, with a better (or at least more self-aware) mind. And by offering that experience rather than another, these works shift the focus of attention from themselves and from what is happening in their formal confines to the reader and what is happening in the confines of his mind and heart.

In terms of the *substance* of his rhetoric/dialectic distinction, I could hardly suggest a better way of describing the difference I see between the parables of the general Jewish tradition and those of Jesus, or between the parables of a Tolstoy and a Kafka. And one recognizes the irony that places Tolstoy with the Talmud and Jesus with Kafka. But I am less than enthusiastic about the *terms* he has chosen with which to categorize that substance. The two terms, rhetoric and dialectic, are so open to different and diverging interpretations that I would be unable to adopt them without always referring to Fish's precise definitions for them were I, for example, to distinguish between rhetorical and dialectical parables.

I would suggest, instead, that the prefix *meta-* be used for any genre of human communication when that genre is deliberately turned on itself in the self-consuming and self-negating way so magnificently exemplified by Fish for seventeenth century English literature. Two things would be gained by this change, at least for me. First, the ambiguity in the meaning of dialectic is avoided. Second, and more important, the prefix meta- can be applied, as it must, to any genre of human speech or communication when it becomes self-negating or self-consuming. Thus, in a way, I am but grafting upon Fish's distinction the terminology coined by Heinz Politzer almost twenty years ago when he said concerning the parables of Kakfa and Camus that (63): "For Camus as for Kafka, the incomprehensible remains incomprehensible, and a paradox takes the place of any rational maxim conveyed by the narration. It is a kind of *meta-didactic* prose: at the core of the secret a new mystery is hidden" (my italics). So, then, parables can be didactic or metadidactic (Politzer), or, there can be rhetorical and dialectical parables (Fish), or, for me, there are both parables and metaparables. And high among the metaparables is that "self-consuming artifact" (Fish), the story of the hidden treasure.

3.332 *Self-Consuming Artifacts*

Jesus' treasure story is thus a metaparable, a paradoxical artifact which succeeds precisely to the extent that it fails. I will tell you, it says, what the Kingdom of God is like. Watch carefully how and as I fail to do so and learn that it cannot be done. Have you seen my failure? If you have, then I have succeeded. And the more magnificent my failure, the greater my success.

I wish to conclude, then, by bringing into contrast with Jesus' metaparable two poems by George Herbert which Fish (173–79) cites to exemplify his thesis concerning "self-consuming artifacts" which effect, in Milton's marvelous phrase (Fish: 75), "a kind of saving by undoing."

The first poem is "The Holdfast" (Hutchinson: 143) which is short enough to be given in full.

I threatened to observe the strict decree
  Of my deare God with all my power & might.
  But I was told by one, it could not be;
Yet I might trust in God to be my light.
Then will I trust, said I, in him alone.
  Nay, ev'n to trust in him, was also his:
  We must confesse that nothing is our own.
Then I confesse that he my succour is:
But to have nought is ours, not to confesse
  That we have nought. I stood amaz'd at this,
  Much troubled, till I heard a friend expresse,
That all things were more our by being his.
  What Adam had, and forfeited for all,
  Christ keepeth now, who cannot fail or fall.

The poem takes speaker and hearer through three backward or downward steps: (1) from observance to trust; (2) from trust to confession; (3) from confession to silence. At which point, like the attentive hearer of Jesus' treasure parable, one can only say, "I stood amaz'd at this." Then the fourth point occurs as Christ, the friend, announces the supreme paradox which consummates the process of "nought" already achieved, by announcing "That all things were more ours by being his." It is important to note, with Fish (176), that the "extraordinary thing about these evasions is that they are moral." What the speaker is holding fast to is such virtues as obedience, trust, and proclamation. "But to have nought is ours, not to confesse / That we have nought." Or, in the image of Jesus' metaparable: one must abandon the abandonment of all one has.

The second poem is an even more striking parallel because it is entitled, "The Pearl. Matth. 13. 45" (Hutchinson: 88–89). It is too long to give here in full so I shall summarize what I want to take from it. One obvious question is why, from my viewpoint, did he choose The Pearl and not The Hidden Treasure, and my only conjecture would be that the problem of the immorality or illegality of the finder's actions was something he wished to avoid as distracting.

The poem has a similar four-point structure to the preceding one. The first stanza begins, "I know the wayes of Learning," then chronicles such knowledge for nine lines before concluding with the brief tenth line, "Yet I love thee." So, also, the second stanza begins, "I know the wayes of Honour," catalogues them for nine lines, and concludes on the tenth, "Yet I love thee." And the third stanza, "I

know the wayes of Pleasure," nine lines of detail, and a terminal
tenth, "Yet I love thee." This, then, is the final verse:

> I know all these, and have them in my hand:
> Therefore not sealed, but with open eyes
> I flie to thee, and fully understand
> Both the main sale, and the commodities;
> And at what rate and price I have thy love;
> With all the circumstances that may move:
> Yet through these labyrinths, not my groveling wit,
> But thy silk twist let down from heav'n to me,
> Did both conduct and teach me, how by it,
>   To climbe to thee.

By the time speaker and reader finished the third and entered the
fourth stanza there was a definite mood of self-sufficient
complacency about giving up the ways of knowledge, honor, and
pleasure, for the higher value of divine love. One had given up all
one's possessions for the desired object. But then even this
abandonment is taken away from the speaker and shown to be
possible only as a gift. As Fish (179) states it, the conclusion "assigns
to that superior value the responsibility for its own recognition."
And, even though the poem ends here,

> the mechanism by which the reader is asked to penetrate to deeper
> and deeper levels of the poem is still operative and pressuring when
> it is formally complete. And moreover, that mechanism is infinitely
> self-perpetuating, for if one must give up the giving up of the world,
> then one must, per force give up the giving up of the giving up, and
> so on in an infinite regress. . . . "The Pearl" is finally a *profoundly*
> unsatisfactory poem, for there is no position one can assume in
> relation to it without compounding and extending the error it
> exposes.

What is happening here is one of the most extraordinary events in
all the world. It is language genuflecting, not just talking about doing
it in content, but actually doing it in form. Hence, what Fish (179)
says of Herbert's poem on "The Pearl" is exactly what I have tried to
say of Jesus' parable on The Hidden Treasure: "The speaker begins
by declaring his willingness to give up all that he has for God and he
ends by giving up the giving up."

WORKS CONSULTED

There are three sections in the Works Consulted. Most references will be to the second one on Treasure Stories. If the reference is not found there, it will be necessary to check the third or the first section, in that order. See conclusion for Abbreviations.

1 MOTIF INDEXES

Aarne, Antti & Stith Thompson
    1961   *The Types of the Folktale.* FFC 184. 2nd rev. Helsinki: Academia Scientiarum Fennica.

Balys, Jonas
    1936   *Motif-Index of Lithuanian Narrative Folk-Lore.* Folk-Lore Studies 2. Kaunas: Publication of the Lithuanian Folk-Lore Archives.

Baughman, Ernest Warren
    1966   *Type and Motif-Index of the Folktales of England and North America.* Indiana University Publications: Folklore Series 20. The Hague: Mouton.

Boberg, Inger M.
    1966   *Motif-Index of Early Icelandic Literature.* Bibliotheca Arnamagnaeana 27. Copenhagen: Munksgaard.

Bødker, Laurits
    1957   *Indian Animal Tales: A Preliminary Survey.* FFC 170. Helsinki: Academia Scientiarum Fennica.

Boggs, Ralph Steele
    1930   *Index of Spanish Folktales.* FFC 90. Helsinki: Academia Scientiarum Fennica.

Bordman, Gerard
    1963   *Motif-Index of the English Metrical Romances.* FFC 190. Helsinki: Academia Scientiarum Fennica.

Christiansen, Reidar Thorwald
    1958   *The Migratory Legends: A Proposed List of Types with a Systematic Catalogue of the Norwegian Variants.* FFC 175. Helsinki: Academia Scientiarum Fennica.

Cross, Tom Peete
    1952   *Motif-Index of Early Irish Literature.* Indiana University Publications: Folklore Series 7. Bloomington, IN: Indiana University Press.

Dundes, Alan
1976 *Folklore Theses and Dissertations in the United States.* Publications of the American Folklore Society: Bibliographical & Special Series 27. Austin: University of Texas Press.

Flowers, Helen Leniva
1952 *A Classification of the Folktales of the West Indies by Types and Motifs.* Ph.D. dissertation at Indiana University.

Ikeda, Hiroko
1971 *A Type and Motif Index of Japanese Folk-Literature.* FFC 209. Helsinki: Academia Scientiarum Fennica.

Keller, John Esten
1949 *Motif-Index of Mediaeval Spanish Exempla.* Knoxville, TN: University of Tennessee Press.

Kirtley, Bacil F.
1971 *A Motif-Index of Traditional Polynesian Narratives.* Honolulu: University of Hawaii Press.

Neuman [Noy], Dov
1954 *Motif-Index of Talmudic-Midrashic Literature.* Ph.D. dissertation at Indiana University.

Nyerges, Anton N.
1952 "The Folktale: Type and Motif Analysis and Index." Pp. 13–114 in *Studies in Cheremis Folklore.* Ed. Thomas A. Sebeok. Indiana University Publications: Folklore Series 6. Bloomington, IN: Indiana University Press.

Rotunda, Dominic Peter
1942 *Motif-Index of the Italian Novella in Prose.* Indiana University Publications: Folklore Series 2. Bloomington, IN: Indiana University Press [Reprinted, New York: Haskell House, 1973].

Simonsuuri, Lauri
1961 *Typen- und Motivverzeichnis der Finnischen Mythischen Sagen.* FFC 182. Helsinki: Academia Scientiarum Fennica.

Thompson, Stith
1929 *Tales of the North American Indians.* Bloomington, IN: Indiana University Press.

Thompson, Stith
1966 *Motif-Index of Folk-Literature.* 6 vols. Revised & Enlarged (1955–58). Bloomington, IN: Indiana University Press.

Thompson, Stith & Jonas Balys
1958 *The Oral Tales of India.* Indiana University Publications: Folklore Series 10. Bloomington, IN: Indiana University Press.

Thompson, Stith & Warren E. Roberts
1960 *Types of Indic Oral Tales: India, Pakistan, Ceylon.* FFC 180. Helsinki: Academia Scientiarum Fennica.

Tubach, Frederic C.
1969   *Index Exemplorum: A Handbook of Medieval Religious Tales.*
        FCC 204. Helsinki: Academia Scientiarum Fennica.

2   TREASURE STORIES

Aarne, Antti
1918   *Estnische Märchen- und Sagenvarianten.* FCC 25. Hamina:
        Suomalaisen Tiedeakatemian Kustantama.
1920   *Finnische Märchenvarianten: Ergänzungsheft I.* FCC 33. Hamina:
        Suomalaisen Tiedeakatemian Kustantama (supplement for 1908–
        18 to FCC 5 [1911]).

Abercromby, John
1889   "Legends from County Meath." *FLJ* 7: 313–14.

Addy, Sidney Oldall
1895   *Household Tales with Other Traditional Remains.* London: Nutt.

Anonymous
1878   "Notes." *FLR* 1:235–45.

Basset, René M. J.
1924–26/27 *Mille et un contes, récits et légendes arabes.* 3 vols. Paris:
        Maisonneuve.

Bin Gorion, Micha Joseph, coll., & Emanuel bin Gorion, ed.
1976   *Mimekor Yisrael: Classical Jewish Folktales.* Trans. I. M. Lask. 3
        vols. Bloomington, IN: Indiana University Press.

Bolte, Johannes & Georg Polívka
1913–31 *Anmerkungen zu den Kinder- und Hausmärchen der Brüder
        Grimm.* 5 vols. Leipzig: Weicher.

Bradley-Birt, Francis Bradley
1920   *Bengal Fairy Tales.* London & New York: Lane.

Braude, W. G. & I. J. Kapstein
1975   *Pesikta de-Rab Kahana.* Philadelphia: Jewish Publication Society
        of America.

Briggs, Katharine M. & Ruth L. Tongue
1965   *Folktales of England.* Folktales of the World. Chicago: University
        of Chicago Press.

Buber, S.
1946   *Midrash Tanhuma.* 2 vols. New York: Sefer.

Busk, Rachel Harriette
1870   *Patrañas; or Spanish Stories, Legendary and Traditional.* London:
        Griffith & Farran.

Carrière, Joseph Médard
1937   *Tales from the French Folk-Lore of Missouri.* Northwestern Uni-
        versity Studies in the Humanities 1. Evanston, IL: Northwestern
        University Press.

Chambers, Robert
    1826   *The Popular Rhymes of Scotland.* Edinburgh: Hunter & Smith.

Chavannes, Édouard
    1910–34   *Cinq cents contes et apologues extraits du Tripiṭaka chinois.* 4 vols.
                Paris: Leroux.

Chŏng, In-Sŏp
    1969   *Folk Tales from Korea.* New York: Greenwood Press.

Christiansen, Reidar Thorwald
    1964   *Folktales of Norway.* Folktales of the World. Chicago: University
                 of Chicago Press.

Clouston, William Alexander
    1887   *Popular Tales and Fictions.* 2 vols. Edinburgh & London:
                 Blackwood.
    1888   *The Book of Noodles.* New York: Armstrong.

Colson, F. H. & G. H. Whitaker, trans. & eds.
    1962   *Philo.* 10 vols. LCL. London: Heinemann.

Conybeare, F.C., trans. & ed.
    1926   *Philostratus: The Life of Apollonius of Tyana.* 2 vols. LCL. New
                 York: Putnam's.

Cowell, Edward Byles *et al.,* eds.
    1895–1907 *The Jataka; or, Stories of the Buddha's Former Births.* 6 vols &
                 index (1913). Cambridge: Cambridge University Press.

Daly, L. W., trans.
    1961   *Aesop Without Morals.* New York: Yoseloff.

Danielson, Larry
    1968   "The Disappearing Treasure." *Indiana Folklore* 1: 28–33.

Davidson, Sarah & Eleanor Phelps
    1937   "Folk Tales from New Goa, India," *JAF* 50: 1–51.

Dégh, Linda
    1965   *Folktales of Hungary.* Trans. Judit Halász. Folktales of the World.
                 Chicago: University of Chicago Press.

Dexter, Wilfrid E.
    1938   *Marathi Folk Tales.* London: Harrap.

Dickey, Lyle A.
    1917   "Stories of Wailua, Kauai." *Twenty-Fifth Annual Report of the
                 Hawaiian Historical Society for the Year 1916.* Honolulu: Paradise
                 of the Pacific Press.

Di Francia, Letterio, ed.
    1930   *Le Cento Novelle Antiche o Libro di Novelle e di bel Parlar
                 Gentile—detto anche Novellino.* Classici Italiani, 2a serie, 45.
                 Turin: Unione Tipografico-Editrice Torinese.

Dobie, J. Frank, ed.
1924/1964   *Legends of Texas*. PTFS 3 (1924). Reprinted, Hatboro, PA: Folklore Associates, 1964.

Dorson, Richard M.
1970   *Jonathan Draws the Long Bow*. New York: Russell & Russell [reprint from 1946].
1975   *Folktales Told Around the World*. Chicago: University of Chicago Press.

Dracott, Alice Elizabeth
1906   *Simla Village Tales*. London: Murray.

Drake, Samuel Adams
1884   *A Book of New England Legends and Folk Lore*. Boston: Roberts.

Driscoll, Charles B.
1930   *Doubloons; The Story of Buried Treasure*. New York: Farrar & Rinehart.

Eberhard, Wolfram
1965   *Folktales of China*. Folktales of the World. Chicago: University of Chicago Press.

Elton, Oliver, trans., & F. York Powell, ed.
1905   *The Nine Books of the Danish History of Saxo Grammaticus*. 2 vols. Anglo Saxon Classics. London: Norroena Society.

Elwin, Verrier
1944   *Folk-Tales of Mahakoshal*. London: Oxford University Press.

Emeneau, M. B.
1944-46   *Kota Texts: Parts I–IV = University of California Publications in Linguistics* 2/1 (1944); 2/2 (1946); 3/1&2 (1946).

Fairclough, H. R., trans. & ed.
1955   *Horace: Satires, Epistles and Ars Poetica*. LCL. London: Heinemann.

Fauset, Arthur Huff
1928   "Tales and Riddles Collected in Philadelphia." *JAF* 41: 529–57.

Foster, George M.
1964   "Treasure Tales, and the Image of the Static Economy in a Mexican Peasant Community." *JAF* 77: 39–44.
1965   "Peasant Society and the Image of the Limited Good." *American Anthropologist* 67: 293–315.

Freedman, H. & M. Simon
1961   *Midrash Rabbah*. 10 vols. London: Soncino.

Frobenius, Leo
1921-28   *Atlantis: Volksmärchen und Volksdichtungen Afrikas*. 12 vols. Jena: Diederich.

128   Finding is the First Act

Fürer-Haimendorf, Christoph von
1943   *The Chenchus: Jungle Folk of the Deccan.* London: Macmillan.

Gardner, Emelyn Elizabeth
1937   *Folklore from the Schoharie Hills, New York.* Ann Arbor, MI: University of Michigan Press.

Gayangos y Arce, Pascuel de, ed.
1884   "Libro de los Enxemplos." Pp. 443–542 in *Escritores en prosa anteriores al siglo XV.* Biblioteca de autores españoles 51. Madrid: Rivadeneyra.

Ginzberg, Louis
1913–28   *Legends of the Jews.* 6 vols. & index (1938). Philadelphia: Jewish Publication Society of America.

Graham, David Crockett
1954   *Songs and Stories of the Ch'uan Miao.* Smithsonian Miscellaneous Collections 123/1. Washington, D.C.: Smithsonian Institute.

Gregory, Lady Isabella Augusta
1970   *Visions and Beliefs in the West of Ireland.* New York: Oxford University Press.

Grierson, George Abraham, ed.
1903–22   *Linguistic Survey of India.* 11 vols. Calcutta: Government Printing Office.

Guillaumont, A. *et al.*, trans. & eds.
1959   *The Gospel according to Thomas.* Leiden: Brill/New York: Harper & Row.

Gutch, Eliza
1901   *County Folk-Lore II.* London: Nutt.

Gwynn, E. J.
1905   "The Three Drinking-Horns of Cormac Ua Cuinn." *Ériu* 2: 186–88.

Hambruch, Paul, ed.
1922   *Malaiische Märchen aus Madagaskar und Insulinde.* Jena: Diederich.

Hankey, Rosalie
1942   "California Ghosts." *CFQ* 1: 155–77.

Hardy, James, ed.
1892–95   *The Denham Tracts.* 2 vols. London: Nutt.

Hardland, Edwin Sidney
n.d.   *English Fairy and Other Folk Tales.* London: Walter Scott [c. 1890].
1914   *The Science of Fairy Tales.* New York: Scribners.

Henderson, William
1879   *Notes on the Folk-Lore of the Northern Counties of England and the Borders.* London: Satchell & Peyton.

Hight, G. A., trans.
1972   *The Saga of Grettir the Strong.* London: Dent.

Hirschberg, Stanislaus
1934   *Schatzglaube und Totenglaube.* Breslau: Priebatsch.

Holder, A.
1967   *Pomponi Porfyrionis Commentum in Horatium Flaccum.*
            Hildesheim: Olms.

Hurley, Gerard T.
1951   "Buried Treasure Tales in America." *Western Folklore* 10: 197–216.

Jegerlehner, Johann
1909   *Sagen aus dem Unterwallis.* Basel: Verlag der Schweizerischen
            Gesellschaft für Volkskunde.
1913   *Sagen und Märchen aus dem Oberwallis.* Basel: Helbing &
            Lichtenhahn.

Jethabhai, Ganeshji
1903   *Indian Folklore.* Limbdi: Dubal.

Jones, Gwyn, trans.
1960   *Egil's Saga.* New York: Syracuse University Press.

Joyce, James
1939/1976   *Finnegans Wake.* New York: Penguin Books.

Kennedy, Patrick
1891   *Legendary Fictions of the Irish Celts.* London & New York:
            Macmillan.

Kittredge, George Lyman
1972   *Witchcraft in Old and New England.* New York: Atheneum [from
            1929].

Knight, Arthur Lee
1913   *Told in the Indian Twilight: Mahratta Fairy Tales.* London: Allen.

Knight, Mabel Frances
1925   "Wampanoag Indian Tales." *JAF* 38: 134–37.

Knowles, James Hinton
1893   *Folk-Tales of Kashmir.* London: Keegan Paul, Trench, Trübner.

Kraemer, Jr., C. J.
1936   *The Complete Works of Horace.* New York: Modern Library.

Lauterbach, J. Z.
1933–35   *Mekilta de-Rabbi Ishmael.* 3 vols. Philadelphia: Jewish Publica-
            tion Society of America.

Legrain, Georges Albert
1914   *Louqsor sans les pharaons: légendes et chansons populaires de la
            haute Égypte.* Brussels & Paris: Vromant.

Littlejohn, E. G.
1924/1964   "Lost Gold of the Llano Country." Pp. 20–23 in *Legends of Texas* [see Dobie].

Lorimer, D. L. R. & E. O. Lorimer
1919   *Persian Tales*. London: Macmillan.

Loth, Agnete, trans. & ed.
1962   "Ectors saga." Pp. 79–186 in *Late Medieval Icelandic Romances I*. Editiones Arnamagnaeanae, Series B, 20. Copenhagen: Munksgaard.
1963   "Sigurdar saga." Pp. 93–259 in *LMIR II*. Ed. Arnam. B21. Copenhagen: Munksgaard.
1964   "Vilhjálms saga." Pp. 1–136 in *LMIR IV*. Ed. Arnam. B23. Copenhagen: Munksgaard.
1965   "Sigrgards saga." Pp. 39–107 in *LMIR V*. Ed. Arnam. B24. Copenhagen: Munksgaard.

MacCulloch, Mary Julia
1922   "Folk-Lore of the Isle of Skye." *Folk-Lore* 33: 307–17.

Magnússon, E. & W. Morris, trans.
1888   *Völsunga Saga: The Story of the Volsungs and Niebelungs, with Certain Songs from the Elder Edda*. London: Walter Scott.

Massignon, Geneviève
1968   *Folktales of France*. Trans. Jacqueline Hyland. Folktales of the World. Chicago: University of Chicago Press.

Meade, Florence O.
1932   "Folk Tales from the Virgin Islands." *JAF* 45: 363–71.

Megas, Georgios A.
1970   *Folktales of Greece*. Folktales of the World. Chicago: University of Chicago Press.

Morris, E. P.
1909   *Horace: The Satires*. New York: American Book Company.

Mukharji, Ram Satya
1904   *Indian Folklore*. Calcutta: Sanyal.

Natesa Sastri, S. M.
1908   *Indian Folk-Tales*. Madras: Guardian Press.

Neely, Charles, coll., & John Webster Spargo, ed.
1938   *Tales and Songs of Southern Illinois*. Menasha, WI: Collegiate Press.

Noy, Dov
1963   *Folktales of Israel*. Folktales of the World. Chicago: University of Chicago Press.

Oesterley, Hermann
1872   *Gesta Romanorum*. Berlin: Weidmann.

O'Grady, Standish H. & Robin Flower, eds.
1926-1953   *Catalogue of Irish Manuscripts in the British Museum.* 3 vols.
             London: Trustees of the British Museum.

O'Sullivan, Sean
1966   *Folktales of Ireland.* Folktales of the World. Chicago: University of
             Chicago Press.

Parker, H.
1910-14   *Village Folk-Tales of Ceylon.* 3 vols. London: Luzac [1=1910;
             2&3=1914].

Parker, Angelina
1923   "Oxfordshire Village Folklore, II." *Folk-Lore* 34: 322-33.

Partridge, J. B.
1912   "Cotswold Place-Lore and Customs." *Folk-Lore* 23: 332-42.

Pauli, Johannes
1924   *Schimpf und Ernst.* Ed. Johannes Bolte. 2 vols. Berlin:
             Stubenrauch.

Penzer, N. M., ed.
1932   *The Pentamerone of Giambattista Basile.* 2 vols. New York:
             Dutton.

Perry, Ben Edwin
1952   *Aesopica.* Vol. 1: Greek and Latin Texts. Urbana, IL: University of
             Illinois Press.
1965   *Babrius and Phaedrus.* LCL. Cambridge, MA: Harvard University
             Press.

Pino-Saavedra, Yolando
1967   *Folktales of Chile.* Folktales of the World. Chicago: University of
             Chicago Press.

Plummer, Charles
1968   *Bethada Náem nErenn: Lives of Irish Saints.* 2 vols. London:
             Oxford University Press [from 1922].

Powell, John U.
1901   "Folklore Notes from Southwest Wilts." *Folk-Lore* 12: 71-83.

Ralston, William R. S.
1873   *Russian Folk-Tales.* London: Smith, Elder & Co.

Roberts, Leonard W.
1955   *South from Hell-fer-Sartin: Kentucky Mountain Folk Tales.*
             Lexington, KY: University of Kentucky Press.

Rudkin, Ethel H.
1933   "Lincolnshire Folklore." *Folk-Lore* 44: 189-214.

Schwab, M.
n.d.   *Le Talmud de Jérusalem.* 6 vols. Paris: Maisonneuve et Larose.

Sikes, Wirt
    1973   *British Goblins.* East Ardsley, Yorkshire: EP Publishing [from 1880].

Simpson, Jacqueline
    1972   *Icelandic Folktales and Legends.* Berkeley & Los Angeles: University of California Press.
    1973   "Sussex Local Legends." *Folklore* 84: 206–23.

Skeat, Walter William
    1967   *Malay Magic.* New York: Dover [from 1900].

Skinner, Charles M.
    1896   *Myths and Legends of Our Own Land.* 2 vols. Philadelphia: Lippincott.
    1903   *American Myths and Legends.* 2 vols. Philadelphia: Lippincott.

Smiley, Portia
    1919   "Folk-Lore from Virginia, South Carolina, Georgia, Alabama, and Florida." *JAF* 32: 357–83.

Smith, Grafton Elliott
    1919   *The Evolution of the Dragon.* London & New York: Longmans, Green.

Steere, Edward
    1869   *Swahili Tales, as Told by Natives of Zanzibar.* London: S.P.C.K.

Stokes, Whitley, trans. & ed.
    1890   *Lives of Saints from the Book of Lismore.* Oxford: Clarendon Press.

Strack, H. L. & P. Billerbeck
    1922–28   *Kommentar zum Neuen Testament aus Talmud und Midrasch.* 4 vols. Munich: Beck.

Sturleson, Snorre
    1844   *The Heimskringla; or, Chronicle of the Kings of Norway.* Trans. Samuel Laing. 3 vols. London: Longman, Brown, Green, & Longmans.

Suplee, Laura M.
    1918   "The Legend of Money Cove." *JAF* 31: 272–73.

Sutherland, Mary A.
    1924 / 1964   "The Dream Woman and the White Rose Bush." Pp. 89–91 in *Legends of Texas* [see Dobie].

Tawney, C. H., trans., & N. M. Penzer, ed.
    1924–28   *The Ocean of Story.* 10 vols. London: Sawyer.

Thompson, Stith
    1951   *The Folktale.* New York: Dryden.

Thorpe, Benjamin
    1851   *Northern Mythology.* 3 vols. London: Lumley.

Tolkien, Christopher
　　1960　　*The Saga of King Heidrek the Wise.* London: Nelson.

Upreti, Gaṅgā Datt
　　1894　　*Proverbs and Folklore of Kumaun and Garhwal.* Lodiana: Lodiana
　　　　　　Mission Press.

Van Gennep, A.
　　1903　　"Les trésors cachés: le meurtre et les trésors." *Revue des traditions
　　　　　　populaires* 18: 418.

Von Blittersdorf, Louis
　　1924/1964　"Buried Treasure Legends of Milam County." Pp. 99–103 in
　　　　　　Legends of Texas [see Dobie].

Wallach, L.
　　1941　　"Alexander the Great and the Indian Gymnosophists in Hebrew
　　　　　　Tradition." *Proceedings of the American Academy for Jewish
　　　　　　Research* 11: 47–83.

Webb, Wheaton P.
　　1945　　"Witches in the Cooper Country." *NYFQ* 1: 5–20.

Werner, E. T. C.
　　1958　　*Myths and Legends of China.* London: Harrap [from 1922].

Westropp, Thomas J.
　　1910–12　"A Folklore Survey of County Clare." *Folk-Lore* 21 (1910) 338–49
　　　　　　& 23 (1912) 204–15.

White, Newman Ivey, gen. ed.
　　1952–61　*The Frank C. Brown Collection of North Carolina Folklore.* 5 vols.
　　　　　　Durham, NC: Duke University Press.

Winter, Leo
　　1925　　*Die deutsche Schatzsage.* Wattenscheid: Busch.

Wood-Martin, W.G.
　　1902　　*Traces of the Elder Faiths of Ireland.* 2 vols. London: Longmans,
　　　　　　Green.

Yelvington, Henry
　　1936　　*Ghost Lore.* San Antonio, TX: Naylor.

3 OTHER STUDIES

Allenbach, J. *et al.*
　　1975　　*Biblia Patristica: Index des citations et allusions bibliques dan la
　　　　　　littérature patristique. Des origines à Clément d'Alexandrie et
　　　　　　Tertullien.* Paris: Éditions du Centre National de la Recherche
　　　　　　Scientifique.

Barthes, Roland
　　1971　　"Action Sequences." Pp. 5–14 in *Patterns of Literary Style.* Ed. J.
　　　　　　Strelka. Yearbook of Comparative Criticism 3. University Park &
　　　　　　London: The Pennsylvania State University Press.

Beardslee, W. A.
    1978   "Parable, Proverb, and Koan." *Semeia* 13: 151–77.

Borges, Jorge Luis
    1964   "The Garden of the Forking Paths." Pp. 19–29 in *Labyrinths*. Eds.
                D. A. Yates & J. A. Irby. New York: New Directions.

Bury, R. G., trans. & ed.
    1926   *Plato: Laws*. 2 vols. LCL. London: Heinemann.

Caillois, Roger
    1961   *Man, Play, and Games*. Trans. Meyer Barash. New York: Crowell-
                Collier (The Free Press of Glencoe).

Calvino, Italo
    1977   *The Castle of Crossed Destinies*. New York: Harcourt Brace
                Jovanovich.

Childs, Brevard S.
    1974   *The Book of Exodus*. The Old Testament Library. Philadelphia:
                Westminster.

Crossan, John Dominic
    1973   *In Parables*. New York: Harper & Row.
    1975   *The Dark Interval*. Niles, IL: Argus Communications.
    1976a   *Raid on the Articulate*. New York: Harper & Row.
    1976b   "Hidden Treasure Parables in Late Antiquity." Pp. 359–79 in *SBL
                1976 Seminar Papers*. Missoula, MT: Scholars Press.
    1977   "A Metamodel for Polyvalent Narration." *Semeia 9: Polyvalent
                Narration*, 105–47.

Daiches, S. & H. Freedman
    1962   *Hebrew-English Edition of the Babylonian Talmud: Baba Meẓiʿa*.
                London: Soncino.

Davies, W. D.
    1976   "From Schweitzer to Scholem: Reflections on Sabbatai Svi." *JBL*
                95: 529–58.

Dehandschutter, B.
    1971   "Les paraboles de l'Évangile selon Thomas. La Parabole du Trésor
                Caché (log. 109)." *ETL* 47: 199–219.

Derrett, J. D. M.
    1970   *Law in the New Testament*. London: Darton, Longman & Todd.
                Pp. 1–16 = "Law in the New Testament: The Treasure in the Field
                (Mt.XIII,44)." *ZNW* 54 (1963) 31–42.

Dickinson, Emily
    1958   *The Letters of Emily Dickinson*. Ed. T. H. Johnson. 3 vols.
                Cambridge, MA: The Belknap Press of Harvard University Press.

Dundes, Alan
    1962a   "From Etic to Emic Units in the Structural Study of Folktales."
                JAF 75: 95–105.

1962b   "The Binary Structure of 'Unsuccessful Repetition' in Lithuanian Folk Tales." *Western Folklore* 21: 165–74.

Edmonton, Munro S.
1971   *Lore: An Introduction to the Science of Folklore and Literature.* New York: Holt, Rinehart & Winston.

Fish, Stanley E.
1972   *Self-Consuming Artifacts.* Berkeley & Los Angeles: University of California Press.

Frye, Northrop
1976   *The Secular Scripture: A Study of the Structure of Romance.* Cambridge, MA: Harvard University Press.

Funk, Robert W.
1975   *Jesus as Precursor.* Semeia Supplements 2. Missoula, MT: Scholars Press / Philadelphia: Fortress Press.

Gager, John G.
1975   *Kingdom and Community.* Englewood Cliffs, NJ: Prentice-Hall.

Gass, W. H.
1970   *Fiction and the Figures of Life.* New York: Knopf.

Halliday, M. A. K.
1964   "The Linguistic Study of Literary Texts." Pp. 302–7 in *Proceedings of the Ninth International Congress of Linguistics, 1962,* Ed. H. G. Hunt. Janua Linguarum, Series Maior 12. The Hague: Mouton.

Heidegger, Martin
1962   "Letter on Humanism." Pp. 270–302 in *Philosophy in the Twentieth Century.* Eds. W. Barrett & H. Aiken. New York: Random House.

Hennecke, Edgar & Wilhelm Schneemelcher
1965   *New Testament Apocrypha.* 2 vols. Philadelphia: Westminster.

Hill, George
1936   *Treasure Trove in Law and Practice.* Oxford: Clarendon Press.

Hutchinson, F. E., ed.
1941   *The Works of George Herbert.* Oxford: Clarendon Press.

Jakobson, Roman
1956   "The Metaphoric and Metonymic Poles." Pp. 76–82 in R. Jakobson and M. Halle, *Fundamentals of Language.* Janua Linguarum, Series Minor 1. The Hague: Mouton.

Jauss, Hans Robert
1970–71   "Literary History as a Challenge to Literary Theory." *New Literary History* 2: 7–37.

Johnston, Robert M.
1976   "The Study of Rabbinic Parables: Some Preliminary Observations." Pp. 337–57 in *1976 SBL Seminar Papers.* Missoula, MT: Scholars Press.

136   Finding is the First Act

Kingsbury, Jack Dean
    1969   *The Parables of Jesus in Matthew 13.* Richmond, VA: John Knox.

Klausner, Joseph
    1926   *Jesus of Nazareth.* Trans. H. Danby. New York: Macmillan.

Lévi, Israel
    1881a   "La légende d'Alexandre dans le Talmud." *Revue des Études Juives*
                2: 293–300.
    1881b   "Les traductions hébraiques de l'histoire légendaire d'Alexandre."
                REJ 3: 238–65.
    1883   "Le légende d'Alexandre dans le Talmud et la Midrasch." *REJ* 7:
                78–93.

Lyons, John
    1971   *Introduction to Theoretical Linguistics.* London: Cambridge Uni-
                versity Press.

Merwin, W. S.
    1977   *Houses and Travellers.* New York: Atheneum.

Perrin, Norman
    1967   *Rediscovering the Teaching of Jesus.* New Testament Library. New
                York: Harper & Row.
    1976   *Jesus and the Language of the Kingdom.* Philadelphia: Fortress
                Press.

Pettit, Philip
    1975   *The Concept of Structuralism: A Critical Analysis.* Berkeley & Los
                Angeles: University of California Press.

Politzer, Heinz
    1960   "Franz Kafka and Albert Camus: Parables for Our Time." *Chicago
                Review* 14/1 (Spring): 47–67.

Ricoeur, Paul
    1975   "The Narrative Form; The Metaphorical Form; The Specificity of
                Religious Language." *Semeia 4: Paul Ricoeur on Biblical
                Hermeneutics,* 29–148.

Roberts, Alexander & James Donaldson
    1926   *The Ante-Nicene Fathers.* 10 vols. New York: Scribner's.

Saussure, Ferdinand de
    1966   *Course in General Linguistics.* New York: McGraw-Hill.

Scholem, Gershom
    1973   *Sabbatai Ṣevi: The Mystical Messiah.* Trans. R. J. Zwi
                Werblowsky. Bollingen Series 93. Princeton, NJ: Princeton
                University Press.

Schwartz, Howard
    1976   *Imperial Messages: One Hundred Modern Parables.* New York:
                Avon Books.

Strack, Hermann L.
1969   *Introduction to the Talmud and Midrash.* New York: Atheneum.

Tannehill, Robert C.
1975   *The Sword of His Mouth.* Semeia Supplements 1. Missoula, MT: Scholars Press / Philadelphia: Fortress Press.

Vawter, Bruce
1977   "Divorce and the New Testament." *CBQ* 39: 528–42.

Via, Jr., Dan O.
1967   *The Parables.* Philadelphia: Fortress Press.
1975   *Kerygma and Comedy in the New Testament.* Philadelphia: Fortress Press.
1976   "Religion and Story: Of Time and Reality." *JR* 56: 392–99.

Wilder, Amos Niven
1974   "The Parable of the Sower: Naivete and Method in Interpretation." *Semeia 2: The Good Samaritan,* 134–51.

ABBREVIATIONS

Besides the standard abbreviations established in *JBL* 95/2 (June, 1976) 335–46, the following ones have been used:

CFQ	*California Folklore Quarterly*
FFC	Folklore Fellows Communications (by No., not Vol.)
FLJ	*Folk-Lore Journal*
FLR	*Folk-Lore Record*
JAF	*Journal of American Folklore*
NYFQ	*New York Folklore Quarterly*
PTFS	Publications of the Texas Folklore Society

INDEX OF AUTHORS

139